THE *Mind* OF THE *Book*

The

MIND *of the* BOOK

Pictorial Title Pages

ALASTAIR FOWLER

OXFORD

UNIVERSITY PRESS

OXFORD
UNIVERSITY PRESS

Great Clarendon Street, Oxford, OX2 6DP,
United Kingdom

Oxford University Press is a department of the University of Oxford.
It furthers the University's objective of excellence in research, scholarship,
and education by publishing worldwide. Oxford is a registered trade mark of
Oxford University Press in the UK and in certain other countries

First Edition published in 2017

Published in the United States of America by Oxford University Press
198 Madison Avenue, New York, NY 10016, United States of America

British Library Cataloguing in Publication Data
Data available

Library of Congress Control Number: 2016948375

ISBN 978–0–19–871766–9

For my son, David

PREFACE

This book began as a response to Marjorie Corbett and Ronald Lightbown's *The Comely Frontispiece* (1979). That inspiring and provocative work appeared before the History of the Book was much written about. So it seemed a worthwhile enterprise to situate the pictorial title page within that history. In the course of exploring this project, two hypotheses emerged. First, that some features of the title page have remained constant, or at least recurrent, over very long periods: author portraits, for example, go back to antiquity, and can still be seen on many dust jackets today. Second, the front matter of books—what is sometimes called paratext—has undergone so many metamorphoses in response to technological change (script to print to mass production), let alone changes of taste and fashion, that it can be hard to recognize the continuities.

In short, title-page forms are so multifarious it would take several tomes to cover them all. This book is only an essay sketching some outstanding topics and illustrating them with plates and attendant commentaries. The hope is to raise interest in frontispieces and title pages usually passed over with a cursory glance. They deserve a closer look, if not quite the intense scrutiny they received in an earlier age, when they were committed to memory.

In what follows, many specialisms are touched on and at least as many debts incurred. If some are not acknowledged, it is not intentional, but merely the result of faulty memory.

Bill Bell first made me aware that the History of the Book had grown to be a distinct discipline of thought. Michael Bath taught the place of inscriptions in decorative art, and much else. John Manning—and other emblem specialists at the 1993 Pittsburgh conference—opened up perspectives on this most elusive of genres. On particular periods, the best guides were, for the seventeenth century, the much missed Robert M. Cummings; for the eighteenth century, Paul Cheshire; and for the nineteenth, Susan Cruikshank. On art-historical matters, and especially on the history of prints and printmaking, the indispensible guide was Michael Bury. The late William Bellamy taught me much about chronograms, and other covert features of title pages.

Dr Emily Goetsch collected images for the illustrations and arranged for permissions. Her contribution was supported in part by the Edinburgh University School of Literature, Languages, and Cultures, who facilitated our work in many ways.

Images from the Trinity College Library Dublin featured in the ebook or electronic publication of this book may not be further reproduced from software. For reproduction, application must be made to the Head of Digital Resources and Imaging Services, by post to Trinity College Library Dublin, College Street, Dublin 2, Ireland; or by email at digitalresources@tcd.ie.

Alastair Fowler

University of Edinburgh
2016

CONTENTS

CONTENTS

LIST OF FIGURES

ABBREVIATIONS

Cave and Ayad	Roderick Cave, and Sara Ayad, *A History of the Book in 100 Books* (London: British Library, 2014)
Corbett and Lightbown	Marjorie Corbett and R. W. Lightbown, *The Comely Frontispiece: The Emblematic Title-page in England 1550–1660* (London: Routledge & Kegan Paul, 1979)
EETS	Early English Texts Society
Herford and Simpson	*Ben Jonson*, ed. C. H. Herford, Percy Simpson, and Evelyn Simpson (Oxford: Clarendon Press, 1925–52)
Hill and Pollard	Sir George F. Hill and Graham Pollard, *Renaissance Medals at the National Gallery of Art* (London: Phaidon for the Samuel H. Kress Foundation, 1967)
Johnson, *Catalogue*	*A Catalogue of Engraved and Etched English Title-Pages down to . . . 1691* (Oxford: Bibliographical Society and Oxford University Press, 1934)
Luborsky and Ingram	Ruth Samson Luborsky and Elizabeth Morley Ingram, *A Guide to English Illustrated Books 1536–1603* (Tempe, AZ: MRTS, 1998)
MRTS	Medieval and Renaissance Text Society
OCB	*Oxford Companion to the Book*
OCD	*Oxford Classical Dictionary*
ODEP	*Oxford Dictionary of English Proverbs*, 3rd edn
OED	*Oxford English Dictionary*
OGCM	*Oxford Guide to Classical Mythology*
OHLTE	*The Oxford History of Literary Translation in English*
OLD	*Oxford Latin Dictionary*
STC	*Short Title Catalogue*
'Twickenham Pope'	Alexander Pope, *Poems*, ed. John Butt et al., 11 vols in 12 (London: Methuen; New Haven: Yale University Press, 1939–69)

Introduction

Historical Setting

In the ancient world texts had no titles in the modern sense, and therefore no title pages. This applied even to the manuscript known as the *Roman Virgil* (AD 470–500), whose only paratexts (preliminaries) are pairs of framed illustrations. Before the *Aeneid*, for example, the surviving illustration immediately before the title page (fo. 77ʳ) represents the storm at sea (*Aeneid* 1.81–123). The first text page (fo. 78ʳ) comprises eighteen lines, majuscules throughout, solely distinguished from following pages by rubrication of the first three lines and enclosure within a roughly executed frame.[1]

In general, titles were of little importance in manuscript books. Throughout the Middle Ages the beginning of a manuscript was usually marked, if at all,

[1] See David H. Wright, *The Roman Vergil and the Origins of Medieval Book Design* (London: British Library, 2001), 27.

3

Fig. 1. *Chi Rho* incipit, *Book of Kells*, MS58, fo. 34ʳ. Courtesy of Trinity College Library Dublin.

only by decoration of the first phrase. This phrase, the *incipit* ('here begins'), was often taken to refer to the manuscript as a whole, much as we use a title.

It was a different matter with sacred scriptures such as the *Book of Kells*, whose pervasive decoration was among the foremost cultural achievements of the period (Fig. 1).

Even considering these and other grand exceptions, R. B. McKerrow was not wrong in his broad generalization that the title page—defined as 'a separate page setting forth in a conspicuous manner the title of the book which follows it, and not containing any part of the text of the book itself' was 'very seldom used in manuscripts before the date of [its] introduction in printed books'.[2] By about 1500, however, some sort of title page was common, even in manuscript books.

The increased use of title pages is now regarded as a consequence of the mass-production methods necessary with printing. Individual manuscripts, being invariably made on commission and produced on a one-off basis, could be bound at once. By contrast, printed books were for economic reasons made in large numbers. About 180 copies were printed of the Gutenberg Bible; of the more than 760 editions of Books of Hours between 1485 and 1530, perhaps 300 of each was printed; and probably as many as 20,000 copies of the 1539 *Great Bible*.[3] The new technology required that copies not immediately sold must be kept unbound, perhaps for years, or else transported in barrels, boxes, chests, or bales to a distant bookseller.[4] A blank leaf at the beginning of the book served to protect it during the interval between printing and sale. This protective blank naturally called for some means of identification, and acquired it at first in a simple label title.

Soon, additional features accrued to the label title. With promotion as the driving force, information about the printer was added. Then, in Venetian title pages of the 1490s, decorative text borders began to be introduced. This

[2] Ronald B. McKerrow, *An Introduction to Bibliography for Literary Students* (Oxford: Clarendon Press, 1927), 88.

[3] Christopher de Hamel, *A History of Illuminated Manuscripts* (1996; rev. edn London: Phaidon, 1997), 176.

[4] See Margaret M. Smith, *The Title-Page: Its Early Development 1460–1510* (London: British Library; New Castle, DE: Oak Knoll Press, 2000), 18.

was not a necessary reform: *incipits* and colophons together were perfectly adequate.[5]

Printed books, however, naturally retained many customary features of the manuscript book: the opening sentence or phrase (now sometimes abbreviated to a title);[6] the *incipit* (often signalled by a large or decorated initial capital); and some sort of framing decoration. Usually, 'a decorative emphasis' passed 'from the opening words of the manuscript text itself to the title and [...] to the identity of the producer' of the book.[7]

Early titles were like *incipits*, running to length and cumbrousness, as in William Caxton's translation of the anonymous *Image du monde*, wrongly attributed to Vincentius. The title of Caxton's *Mirrour of the World* (1481) is embedded in a wordy *incipit*:

Here begynneth the table of the rubrics of this present volume named the Mirrour of the world or thymage of the same. The prologue declareth to whom this volume apperteyneth and at whos reequeste it was translated out of French in to englissh. After foloweth the prologue of the translatour declarying the substaunce of this present volume. After foloweth the book called the Myrour of the world and speketh first of the power and puissance of God.

Reducing such preambles to brief, sometimes very brief, titles called for careful thought and sometimes an attempt at wit.

Soon this led to more consciously contrived titles, of poems as well as books. The poem titles in George Gascoigne's *A Hundreth Sundrie Flowres* (1573) show this development in progress. Some are external and descriptive: 'An absent lover doth thus encourage his Lady'; 'Three Sonets in sequence'. Others, such as 'Gascoigns Anatomie' and 'Gascoignes wodmanship', seem more integrated, more incorporated with the poems they designate.

This development went beyond conventions of presentation. The very concept of titling was itself in process of change. By the seventeenth century,

---

[5] For a fuller account, see Smith, *Title-Page*, 18–26; Alfred William Pollard, *Titles and Colophons: Last Words on the History of the [Early] Title-Page with Notes on Some Colophons* (London: Nimmo, 1891; repr. Charleston, SC: Bibliobazaar, 2015).

[6] On the matter of abbreviation, see Walter J. Ong, SJ, *Ramus, Method, and the Decay of Dialogue* (Cambridge, MA: Harvard University Press, 1958); Smith, *Title-Page*, 22, 27.

[7] Ibid. 23.

many poets regarded titles as opportunities for a new sort of wit. Several of George Herbert's poem titles now appear far-fetched to the point of obscurity. Or they may allude to emblems, as in 'The Pulley'. With books, such titling might depend on allusions similarly far-fetched. The relevance of Hobbes's title *Leviathan*, for example, is far from obvious, even when its biblical allusion is explained.[8] In Isaiah 27: 1, Leviathan is 'that crooked serpent', identified with 'the dragon that is in the sea'; but, in Psalm 104: 26, Leviathan is 'whom thou [God] hast made to play therein'. As we shall see, Hobbes intends a figure of the state in both benign and dangerous aspects, which sovereignty must control.

Eleanor Shevlin places the title's coming of age in the eighteenth century, when it first 'participates in the world outside' the text.[9] But the many seventeenth-century instances of witty titling suggest that this view needs revision.

In the fifteenth-century transition from manuscript to print, various false starts and short-lived forms of title page can be discerned. Among such transitional forms may be mentioned end-titles; hand-illuminated printed texts (especially initial capitals); and rubricated *incipits*, as in the Gutenberg Bible. But these lie outside our present concerns; and the reader must be referred for them to Margaret Smith's fuller account with its supporting statistical analyses.[10]

For the most part, the elements of the printed title page already occurred in manuscript books. This should not be altogether attributed to inertia (although there was plenty of that). The manuscript book, being a luxury form far superior at first to almost anything in print, inevitably determined expectations of what a book should look like. Besides typographic ornamentation such as large-size lettering and patterned layouts,[11] sixteenth-century

---

[8] On the literary development of titling, see Harry Levin, 'The Title as a Literary Genre', *MLR* 72 (1977), pp. xxiii–xxxvi; Alastair Fowler, *Kinds of Literature: An Introduction to the Theory of Genres and Modes* (Oxford: Clarendon Press; Cambridge, MA: Harvard University Press, 1982; repr. 1985), 92–8.

[9] Eleanor F. Shevlin, ' "To Reconcile Book and Title, and Make 'em Kin to One Another", The Evolution of the Title's Contractual Functions', *Book History*, 2 (1999), 42–77.

[10] See Smith, *Title-Page*, 59–109.

[11] Taken over from the manuscript book; see ibid., index, s.v. *diamond-shaped layout; half-diamond indentation*; Theodore Low de Vinne, *A Treatise on Title-Pages with Numerous Illustrations in Facsimile and some Observations on the Early and Recent Printing of Books* (New York: Century Co., 1902), 13–19.

printed title pages were decorated like presentation manuscripts in at least five ways discussed below. They might have (1) decorated borders like those in manuscript Books of Hours; (2) a framing structure, commonly architectural, with columns, plinths, arches, and aedicules; (3) an author portrait, at first like its simple antique predecessors but now often framed within a medallion or cartouche; (4) a printer's device, often a rebus; (5) a tableau of emblematic figures; (6) an epigraph, sometimes concealing a chronogram; and (7) compartments containing vignettes or symbols summarizing the contents to follow.

Borders

Book margins have always been used for marginalia of many sorts. Authors have systematically appropriated the space for their references, and readers have used it for augmenting or criticizing the text.[1] With few exceptions, decorative borders surrounding the text were at first introduced only in religious works such as bibles and calendars. In secular books, they developed only in the Renaissance or late Middle Ages.

From an early date, borders of various sorts appear in literary manuscripts. The simplest form, a linear frame, already encloses the illustrations of both the *Roman Vergil* and the *Vatican Vergil*.[2] And the first page of the *Aeneid* in

---

[1] On the opportunistic appropriation of marginal spaces by readers, see William H. Sherman, *Used Books: Marking Readers in Renaissance England* (Philadelphia, PA: University of Pennsylvania Press, 2008).

[2] See David H. Wright, *The Roman Vergil and the Origins of Medieval Book Design* (London: British Library, 2001), 16–35.

the *Roman Vergil* has a more elaborate frame using motifs with elements drawn from wall decoration.[3]

By the second half of the seventh century AD, in *The Book of Durrow*, ruled frames now enclosed elaborate carpet pages of interlace.[4] Similarly with the magnificent, early ninth-century *Book of Kells*, where the Gospels are prefaced by preliminary texts, the *breves causae* or summaries of chapter contents and the *argumenta* or prefaces characterizing each evangelist. The *breves causae* of the first three chapters of Matthew give a full-page account of Jesus' birth: *Nativitas Christi in Bethlem iudeae magi munera offerunt et infants interficiuntur regressio.* This complex page presents a sophisticated amalgam of lettering and decoration, with the interlace border (itself framed) morphing into the first upright of the *N* of *Nativitas*.[5]

By the fifteenth century, borders of a very different kind occupied many pages of the *Horae* or Books of Hours. These popular family possessions constituted a large part of manuscript output. When printing was invented, at least 760 separate printed editions of Books of Hours were published between 1485 and 1530. And probably even more were produced by hand than by printing press, since more manuscript copies than printed versions have survived.[6] Such manuscripts presumably formed expectations of what the first generation of early printed books should look like.

Particularly in the Netherlands, fifteenth-century borders often replaced abstract interlace decoration with closely observed images of nature. Such naturalistic botanical and animal imagery increasingly competed for attention with the text. This is particularly striking in the calendars accompanying Hours of the Virgin, which had borders crammed with genre scenes of all kinds. Often these accorded with the season; then they resembled Occupations of the Months. Framing a December or January calendar page there might be scenes of people feasting, or putti snowballing.[7] Sometimes rivalry between

---

[3] fo. 78[r]: Wright, *Roman Vergil*, 27.

[4] See Christopher de Hamel, *A History of Illuminated Manuscripts* (1996; rev. edn London: Phaidon, 1997), pl. 13; Bernard Meehan (ed.), *The Book of Durrow: A Medieval Masterpiece at Trinity College Dublin* (Dublin: Town House, 1996), fos 124[v], 125[v].

[5] Bernard Meehan (ed.), *The Book of Kells* (London: Thames and Hudson, 2012), fo. 8[r], pl. 34.

[6] De Hamel, *A History*, 176.

[7] e.g. Simon Bening's January (*c.*1540), Bayerische Statsbibliothek, reproduced in Ariane van Suchtelen (ed.), *Holland Frozen in Time*, Art Catalogue (The Hague: Mauritshuis with Waanders, Zwolle, 2001–2), pl. 27, p. 38.

text and border amounted to a *paragone* of artist and calligrapher: in the *Mira Calligraphiae* (*c.*1561–2) the illuminator took up themes of the text and carried them to visionary heights.

In Books of Hours, borders often prompted the exercise of memory art. In *The Hours of Catherine of Cleves* (*c.*1440), for example, a border of realistically portrayed coins alludes to the trope whereby memorizing lays up coins in the treasury of memory (Fig. 2). And another border in the same Book of Hours presents fish linked together in a chain and drawn by the hooks of memory (Fig. 3).[8]

By the sixteenth century, such didactic images seem to have been felt as clichés. At any rate, they do not appear in early modern paratexts; although, as we shall see, artificial memory continued to mould pictorial title pages in other ways. Borders in religious books now relied more on biblical images, while those in more worldly books explored mythology, retelling perhaps the exploits of *amorini*. Many title borders were openly secular, even pagan—swarming with *amorini*, dolphins, antique vases, cornucopias, medallion heads, wreaths, and achievements of arms and weapons.[9] Medieval interlace survived in a popular type of frontispiece produced in Venice in the 1490s, in which the border interwove white vine-stems combined with fantasy animals, Cupids, or coats of arms.[10]

Similar borders, designed as woodcuts, were used and reused in printed frontispieces. The earliest examples reflecting a revival of classical ornament were Italian, and most often Venetian, like the famous border used by Gregorius de Rusconibus to frame the first page of St Jerome's *Commentary on Psalms* (Venice, 1498). Despite the Christian character of the text, the motifs of Gregorius' border are classical throughout: vases, cornucopias, floral arrangements, and pagan sacrifice.[11]

By the time of Daniel Hopfer's 1516 Augsburg title page the antique ornament had been interpreted in a more grotesque, neo-Gothic mode: the putti struggle with monsters and entangling acanthus. And in the same year a

[8] Mary J. Carruthers, *The Book of Memory: A Study of Memory in Medieval Culture* (Cambridge: Cambridge University Press, 1990), pls 27, 28.

[9] Ibid. 138; Arthur M. Hind, *An Introduction to a History of Woodcut* (repr. New York: Dover, 1963), type A 1–5.

[10] See Smith, *Title-Page*, 128.

[11] Facsimile in Alexander Nesbitt, *200 Decorative Title-Pages* (1964), pl. 4.

Fig. 2. Treasury of memory, *Hours of Catherine of Cleves*. St. Gregory. Utrecht, the Netherlands, *c.*1440. The Pierpont Morgan Library, New York. MS.917/945, p. 240. Purchased on the Belle da Costa Greene Fund and with the assistance of the Fellows, 1963.

Fig. 3. Hooks of memory, *Hours of Catherine of Cleves*. St Lawrence. Utrecht, the Netherlands, *c.*1440. The Pierpont Morgan Library, New York. MS.917/945, p. 266. Purchased on the Belle da Costa Greene Fund and with the assistance of the Fellows, 1963.

woodcut design by Hans Holbein the Younger has putti clambering over an elaborate niche to support a cloth printed with the title of a commentary on St Paul by Martinus Dorpius, a correspondent of Erasmus. In France, such developments came later. There, a pieced woodcut title border of vases and grotesques by Geoffrey Tory for Rudolph Agricola's *De inventione dialectica* (Paris, 1529) continued the linear, Venetian style. And in 1534 Simon de Colines still used an interlace border for the title page of an astronomical work by Oronce Finé.[12] Meanwhile, German title borders were far grander, not to say grandiose, although often full of intricate details.

By comparison with these continental examples, the title border to *The Workes of Geffray Chaucer* (1532), printed by Thomas Godfray for William Thynne, may seem naive and crudely drawn (Frontispiece 1; p. 72). But this crudeness is the effect of wear. Godfray was reusing a popular, often repaired, border by Holbein himself.[13]

---

[12] Nesbitt, *200 Decorative Title-Pages*, pls 13, 14, 30, 36.

[13] *The Grolier Club's Catalogue of Original and Early Editions of Some of the Poetical and Prose Works of English Writers from Langland to Prior*, 4 vols in 1 (Holland Press, 1964), fig. 39.

Architectural Structures

Renaissance frontispieces often had architectural layouts, or at least layouts using architectural motifs. Indeed, Marjorie Corbett's account of them is largely based on the iconography of classical monuments. She sees the main features as

> the arch or pediment, the flanking columns which enclose the title, the bases or the continuous plinth on which the columns rest. This design is eminently suitable for its purpose; the symmetrical layout gives a telling value to the page, whatever its size, the bold central frame enhances the importance of the title, there is space above and below in the arch or on the plinths for other information.[1]

Such layouts began, in Corbett's view, with fifteenth-century illuminated manuscripts. At a time when classical texts were first being edited by humanist

---

[1] Marjorie Corbett, 'The Architectural Title-Page', *Motif*, 12 (1964), 48–62.

scholars, scribes began to study the inscriptions encountered in monumental settings. Epigraphs in particular were most easily available as 'inscriptions on sarcophagi, grave altars and cinerary urns'—from where Ciriaco of Ancona and others collected them. Hence the prominence of such monuments in manuscript title pages. The title of the *Life of St Onophrius*, for example, appears on the short face of a sarcophagus. If the meaning of 'architecture' is stretched a little, architectural title pages were everywhere in the 1470s—in *The Strozzi Hours*, for example. Or in the *Chronicles of Eusebius*, where the opening words are suspended between two columns.[2]

The garlands, ribbons, and streamers ubiquitous in early frontispieces suggest a different origin: festive decoration. And Corbett even has doubts about the architecture; as when she writes of the *Mirandola Book of Hours*: 'this extravagant little miniature is a pretty jewel in its own right, but it denies the principles of architectural design.'[3] The frontispiece is like architecture, yet unlike it. This apparent paradox lies at the heart of frontispiece design. Many frontispieces—perhaps the majority—present an architecture far from that of real buildings. Think of the woodcut title page of Boccaccio's *Decameron* (Venice, 1492), where the flanking columns are supported on the backs of two surprised-looking lions.[4] Such 'architecture' was not that of stone façades but of stage sets. Indeed, *frontispiece* itself, besides meaning 'façade', meant 'front scenery' or 'the forepart of the stage'.[5] For the origin of a great many frontispiece designs one has to look to the temporary, festal architecture of the theatre, and especially street theatre.

The main pageant structure was called *pegma* or *pegme*, defined in *OED* as 'movable stage or scaffold in a theatre. A kind of framework or stage used in theatrical displays or pageants, sometimes bearing an inscription.'

Ben Jonson uses the word in his description of *Part of King James his Royal and Magnificent Entertainment* (1604): 'The pegme at Fenchurch presented itself in a square and flat upright, like to the side of a city; the top thereof, above the vent and crest, adorned with houses, towers, and steeples set off in perspective. Upon the battlement in a great capital letter was inscribed

---

[2] Corbett, 'Architectural Title-Page', 50, fig. 6; 57, fig. 16.

[3] Ibid. 58, fig. 17.

[4] Cf. Alexander Nesbitt, *200 Decorative Title-Pages* (New York: Dover, 1964), pl. 101, with columns resting on strapwork, and pl. 42, columns resting on sphinxes.

[5] *OED*, sb. 5 b, citing J. Wilson, *Astraea* (London, 1651).

Fig. 4. *Temple of Janus*, Harrison, *Arches of Triumph* (1604). Gough Lond. 145. Courtesy of the Bodleian Libraries, The University of Oxford.

LONDINIUM' (Fig. 4).[6] Beneath were several other inscriptions, such as CAMERA REGIA ('the King's chamber', a traditional designation of London). The major inscription is centred in Jonson's text as in the pegme:

---

[6] Ben Jonson, *Works*, ed. David Bevington et al., 7 vols (Cambridge: Cambridge University Press, 2012), ii. 431–2.

In the centre or midst of the pegme, there was an aback or square, wherein this elogy [explanatory inscription] was written: *Maximus hic rex est, et luce serenior ipsa | Principe quae talem cernit in urbe ducem; | Cuius fortunam superat sic unica virtus* ('This is the greatest king, and the more happy by the light which sees such a leader in his principal city; he is unique in that his unparalleled virtue rises above his fortune') [...][7]

The word *Pegme* has been explained as Jonson's coinage from Greek *pegma*— improbably, since Latin *pegma* was familiar to educated readers of the time from its use by Martial, Seneca, and Pliny the Younger. It was also in Thomas Elyot's Latin *Dictionary* of 1538 and Thomas Cooper's Latin *Dictionary* of 1578: '*Pegma*: a stage or frame whereon pageants be set.' (Jonson has similarly been credited with coining *elogy*; but Latin *elogium* was current from the 1570s.)

George Kernodle's history of show architecture and scenic backgrounds traces early modern developments throughout western Europe: the Terentian stage, the Jesuit façade, the Rederyker stage of the rhetoric societies in the Low Countries, the Elizabethan pageant, and the illusionistic perspective stage. In all likelihood such pegmes provided articulary members for the pictorial frontispieces of sixteenth-century manuscripts and printed books. The temporary structures of festive architecture consisted mainly of wood and cloth. And that is just what many frontispieces and title pages show: flimsy pegmes supporting cloths. These cloths or scrolls or panels, suspended from the frame or held by human agents, display necessary inscriptions: the title, often the author, and sometimes the imprint.

Inscribed cloths can be traced without a break from manuscript opening pages to printed title pages. Intermediate examples prove this point. In a late-fifteenth-century manuscript of Aristotle's *Physics*, the opening page is written on distressed parchment, a worn and curled scroll mounted on a panel which in turn is supported on a plinth, with flanking columns and bases.[8] The opulent Ugelheimer Justinian (Venice, 1477) has similarly worn scrolls for the opening of a section (fo. 2[r], *Incipit liber xxxix digestorum*); yet it was

---

[7] Jonson, *Works*, ii. 439–40.

[8] Vienna Österreichische National Bibliothek, cod. phil. gr. 2; illus. in Jonathan J. G. Alexander, *The Painted Page: Italian Renaissance Book Illumination 1450–1550* (New York: Prestel, 1994), 126, pl. 53.

printed on parchment by Nicolaus Jensen (Fig. 5). The full page of two columns of old parchment is *trompe l'œil*, so torn that a putto appears through one tear, while another reveals a *tableau vivant*, partly obscured by a fragment of text in a different size of type and with an illuminated initial. Four putti hold all this in front of an architectural façade.[9] In Renaissance Italy such witty conflations of script and print, old and new, characterized luxury manuscripts for aristocratic patrons.

In later printed books—even as late as the seventeenth century—titles still appeared on cloths or scrolls supported by putti or fixed to a pegme. Among many examples, the title of William Browne's *Britannia's Pastorals* (1613) is on a fringed cloth suspended by putti; H. Holcroft's 1653 translation of Procopius' *History of Justinian* shows a cloth announcing author, title, and translator, fastened to an arcade, below a bust of Justinian; and, in Palladio's *The First Book of Architecture* translated by G. Richards (1668), putti hold a cloth inscribed with the title, whereas information about the printer (more permanent than any particular title) occupies the plinth.[10]

The title cloth and the means of its suspension varied. In L. de Gand's *Parallelum Olivae* (1656) a scroll is pinned to a stele; in C. Beck's *The Universall Character* (1657) it is tied to pilasters;[11] in J. Rea's *Flora, Ceres, and Pomona* (1665) a fringed and tasselled cloth is tied, aptly, to staples in a garden wall; and in Taylor the Water Poet's *Workes* (1630) author and title are displayed on the bunt of a square sail edged with rope. The god of eloquence himself supports an inscribed cloth announcing T. Blount's *The Arcade of Eloquence* (1654), and a scroll for James Howell's *Familiar Letters* (1645). Occasionally the cloth's support raises questions of fictive status, as in the frontispiece of P. Scarron's *Comical Romance of a Company of Stage Players* (1676), where the inscribed cloth is a fringed theatrical curtain pegged to the page itself, with the peg overlapping the frame of the engraving; although the imprint ('printed by J. C. for W. Crooke') lies outside the frame.[12]

Animal skin might be substituted for cloth. In the frontispiece of Richard Tomlinson's translation of Remodaeus' *Pharmacy* (1657), author, title, and

---

[9] Ibid. 193–5, pl. 97.
[10] Johnson, *Catalogue*, Hole 12; Cross 15; Chantry 4.
[11] Ibid., Faithorne 9, 11; Loggan 4; Cockson 5; Faithorne 6; Marshall 94; Faithorne 20.
[12] Ibid., Faithorne 20.

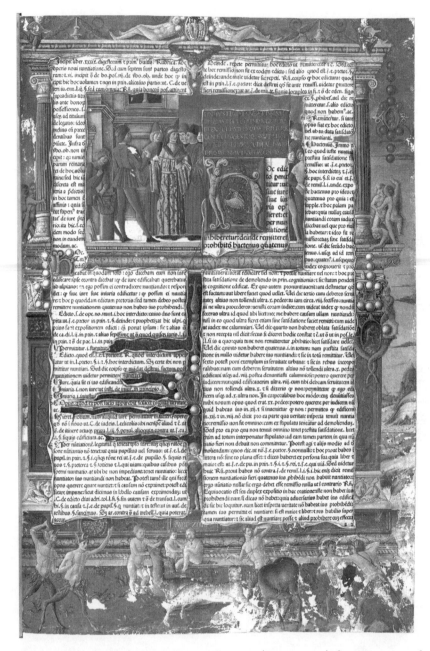

Fig. 5. Manuscript and print, Justinian, *Digestum* (Venice, 1477), fo. 2ʳ. Courtesy of Gotha Research Library, Universität Erfurt.

translator appear on a bear hide supported by Galen and Hippocrates. In E. Warcupp's *Italy* (1660), Hercules indicates the title on his lion skin. And in Francis Barlow's *Diversae avium species* (1658) a deerskin (announcing title, artist, and engraver) is gripped in the beaks of eagles.[13]

All the sorts of pegme described in Kernodle's history appear in early modern title pages: the façade, the arcade of honour, the triumphal arch, and the *tableau vivant* of mythological personages or moral personifications. The commonest is probably the *tableau vivant*, occurring in the title pages of many Bibles, such as the King James Bible of 1611. Printed by the King's Printer Robert Barker, this may be the only work in England by the Amsterdam engraver Cornelis Boel (b. 1580). In it, a *tableau vivant* of Apostles is seated on an arcade, with Moses and Aaron in niches, and Sts Luke and James seated on the bases.[14] Such *tableaux* can be seen in many of Johnson's facsimiles.[15] Almost as frequent are triumphal arches and arcades (Fig. 4).[16]

Show architecture was especially appropriate for the title pages of books conceived as theatres, on the strength of the ancient sense of *theatrum*: 'a field in which one's qualities are exhibited publicly'.[17] Thomas Cooper's *Dictionary* defined *ingenii theatrum* as 'a place or matter wherein one sheweth and declareth his witte'; and John Florio glossed *theatro* as 'a stage or skaffold. Also any spectacle or common display.'

The book as theatre is the subject of Ann Blair's important study *The Theatre of Nature*. She finds her point of departure as early as 1564 in Ronsard and his sources: 'The world is a theatre, men are the actors, fortune is the stage director.'[18]

[13] Johnson, *Catalogue*, Cross 20; Loggan 1; Gaywood 9.

[14] See David Norton, *A Textual History of the King James Bible* (Cambridge: Cambridge University Press, 2005), 46, 64, 66.

[15] e.g. Johnson, *Catalogue*, Cross 15; Delaram 3, 4; Elstrack 5, 6, 10, 13, 15, 23; Faithorne 6, 9, 11; Hole 10; Loggan 4; Marshall 48, 94.

[16] e.g. ibid.: arches: van Dalen 4, Delaram 6, Elstrack 23, Hole 10; arcades: Cecill 16, Marshall 19.

[17] *OLD*, s.v. *Theatrum*, 2; Thomas Cooper, *Thesaurus linguae Romanae et Britannicae* (1578; facsimile edn, Hildesheim and New York: Olms, 1975); John Florio, *Queen Anna's New World of Words* (1611; facsimile edn, Menston: Scolar, 1968), 562.

[18] Ann Blair, *The Theatre of Nature: Jean Bodin and Renaissance Science* (Princeton: Princeton University Press, 1997); cf. E. R. Curtius, 'Metaphorics: Theatrical Metaphors', in *European Literature and the Latin Middle Ages*, trans. Willard R. Trask (London: Routledge & Kegan Paul, 1953), 138–44; William N. West, *Theatres and Encyclopedias in Early Modern Europe* (Cambridge: Cambridge University Press, 2002).

Jean Bodin's influential *Universae naturae theatrum* (1596) encouraged scientific and political applications of the metaphor, while Blair shows that many scientific titles used *theatrum* in the same way: notably Antonius Deusing's *Naturae theatrum universale* (1644), Samuel Purchas's *Theatre of Political Flying-Insects* (1657), Carolus Grueber's *Theatrum naturae* (1672), and Jan Jonston's *Theatrum universale omnium animalium* (1718).[19] Others might be added, such as Ortelius' *Theatrum orbis terrarum* (1570), Speed's *Theatre of the Empire of Great Britain* (1611), and Edward Phillips's *Theatrum poetarum anglicanorum* (1675). More than twenty-eight titles using *theatrum*, *theatre*, and so on appeared before 1700. The use of *theatrum* for a table of contents is particularly suggestive, in view of the many memorial title pages listing contents.[20]

We have been looking at structures characteristic of show architecture. We should also consider a feature equally common in real architecture: the portal. The central bay of a frontispiece arcade or façade, for example, often contained a doorway. In Hollar's frontispiece to Talon's *The Holy History* (1653), Moses sits outside a doorway opening on a receding church interior with an apse. The title is inscribed above the door: on the door case appears the epigraph PER SPECULUM IN AENIGMATE OMNIA IN FIGURIS, adapted from Vulgate 1 Cor. 13: 12 (*Videmus nunc per speculum in aenigmate, tunc autem facie ad faciem*, 'now we see through a glass, darkly; but then face to face'). The personification of faith holds a mirror and points through the door; while on the steps appears the inscription FIDE INVISIBILEM VIDENS MOYSES TANQUAM SUSTINUIT ('seeing through faith the invisible world, Moses endured'). Many architectural frontispieces suggested metaphors like these, of entry into the book they named and introduced. They figured initiation into its intellectual world.

Generally, a frontispiece portal took the form of a triumphal arch. Whereas with real architecture it is imaginable to pass through such an arch, this is not so in a frontispiece. There, entry is blocked by the title inscription and by the unbroken plinth. Readers inescapably come up against the figurative character of the arch. To proceed, they must enter into the book by reading it—by imagining the contents beyond the frontispiece.

[19] Blair, *Theatre of Nature*, 159–66. For further examples, see A. F. Allison and V. F. Goldsmith (eds), *Titles of English Books*, 2 vols (Folkestone: Dawson, 1976), ii. 276.
[20] Blair, *Theatre of Nature*, 161–3.

Portraits

The tradition of picturing authors goes back at least to the sixth century BC, when statues of poets were located at Greek temples. In the second century BC Pausanius recorded statues of Homer and Hesiod, active perhaps 100 years earlier. A statue of Anacreon in his cups was on the Akropolis. And busts of Homer and Euripides actually survive, albeit in Roman copies of Hellenistic originals.

Romans collected statues of Greek but not of Roman writers: they preferred generals and emperors. The earliest surviving representation of the poet Virgil is a Tunisian mosaic of the first or second century AD. It tells almost nothing of his appearance, being a generic representation of a writer, scroll on lap, seated by a reading desk, and flanked by two Muse-like figures (narrative and dramatic literature?). This type was endlessly repeated in ancient portraiture:[1] in the Vienna Dioscorides (*c.*512) the author works on a codex, while his miniaturist paints a mandrake specimen.[2]

The practice of including author portraits in literary manuscripts has been remarkably continuous, from the *Roman Vergil* (AD 470–500) onwards. There we find three portraits of Virgil, two in Eclogues 2 and 4 (monologues) and one in Eclogue 6 (where the poet speaks with his patron Varus).[3] Probably following earlier models, these are still general-purpose author portraits. The featureless poet sits staring straight ahead, holding a scroll and flanked by the professional writer's attributes: a writing desk and a *capsa* or cylindrical scroll-case (Fig. 6). The tradition continued into the Middle Ages and beyond:[4] the Dioscorides portrait may be compared with one of Pliny the Elder presenting his *Historia naturalis* to the Emperor Titus, in the thirteenth century.[5]

Author portraits featured prominently in religious books. One has only to think of the evangelists' images—in *The Book of Lindisfarne* (*c.*698), the Canterbury *Codex aureus* (mid-eighth century), the Godescalc gospels (781–3), the Vienna Coronation gospels (before 800), and the magnificent *Book of Kells* (*c.*800)—to see that the author-portrait convention still regularly applied in Bibles and gospel books (Fig. 7). Yet it also varied widely in variety and style. The Celtic author portraits—abstract, differing little in mode between the evangelists and their symbols—belong to a different cultural world from the comparatively realistic portraits of the Godescalc gospels.

It is much the same with early psalters. (Psalters might then contain the books of the Bible before Psalms.) The eighth-century Vespasian Psalter has a full-page portrait of King David holding a musical instrument.[6] More often the psalmist appears within the counter of an initial letter, as in the NLS *Iona Psalter* of about 1200.

---

[1] David Piper, *The English Face* (London: Thames & Hudson, 1957); *The Image of the Poet: British Poets and their Portraits* (Oxford: Clarendon Press, 1982), 8.
[2] Ingo F. Walther and Norbert Wolf, *Codices Illustres: The World's Most Famous Illuminated Manuscripts 400 to 1600* (Cologne: Taschen, 2001), 56.
[3] David H. Wright, *The Roman Vergil and the Origins of Medieval Book Design* (London: British Library, 2001), 17, 18, 20, 62.
[4] Ibid. 52, 63. [5] Walther and Wolf, *Codices Illustres*, 22.
[6] BL MS Cotton Vespasian A.I, illus. in Christopher de Hamel, *A History of Illuminated Manuscripts* (1996; rev. edn, London: Phaidon, 1997), pl. 7; Ps 97.

Fig. 6. Author portrait, Vergilius Romanus, Vat. Lat. 3867, fo. 14ʳ. Courtesy of the Biblioteca Apostolica Vaticana.

About 1325 Petrarch commissioned a manuscript of Virgil, and about 1340 had a frontispiece painted for it by Simone Martini. This shows epic, georgic, and pastoral figures looking at Virgil their author, who meditates with pen in hand.[7]

As we have seen, early author portraits seldom attempted outward likenesses. At most, they might try to convey a tradition of moral character. And usually they were too generalized even for this. In the fifteenth century, however, a wish arose to put on record what an author actually looked like. About 1412 Thomas Hoccleve inserted in the manuscript of *The Regiment of Princes* a commissioned portrait of Chaucer:

[7] See ibid., pl. 214.

Fig. 7. Evangelist portrait, *Book of Kells*, MS 58 fo. 291ʳ. Courtesy of Trinity College Library Dublin.

> to putte other men in remembrance
> Of his persone I have here his lyknesse
> Do make, to this ende, in sothfastnesse,
> That thei that have of him lest thought and mynde
> By this peynture may ageyn him fynde.
>
> (*Regiment*, 4994–8: BM MS Harley
> 4866, fo. 88ʳ)

In a verse caption, Hoccleve adds that he aimed 'to preserve Chaucer's memory in "soothfastnesse" [truthfulness] lest it fade'.[8] It is one of the earliest likenesses of an English poet, and reflects a new sense of individual authorship.[9]

A slightly earlier representation of Chaucer the pilgrim has been inserted in the Ellesmere MS of *The Canterbury Tales*, in the margin at the beginning of his tale of *Melibee*. Possibly traced from the *Regiment* portrait, it shows Chaucer as a portly figure with a short, forked beard, a pen-case hung round his neck.[10] A manuscript of *Troilus and Criseyde* (*c.*1410–20) has a frontispiece showing Chaucer reading to the court of Richard II—an outdoor scene sometimes too literally interpreted as referring to an actual occasion.[11] And miniature portraits occur in the historiated initial *W* on the first leaf of several manuscripts of *The Canterbury Tales*: apparently a conventional location for such author portraits.[12] Altogether, more than fourteen manuscript portraits of Chaucer are known, some no longer extant. Derek Pearsall lists and dates them in the appendix to his *Life* of Chaucer. A lost manuscript portrait was probably the basis of the first printed one, in Thomas Speght's 1598 edition of the *Works*. With the many 'library portraits' and manuscript portraits inserted later, we are not concerned.[13]

In the early Renaissance, a desire for authentic particularity arose—for example, in Dante portraiture.[14] And an individualized portrait of Chaucer's contemporary John Gower represents him as Amans in *Confessio amantis*.[15] The convention of author portraits continued in printed books, at first with a distinct loss of quality. Woodcuts were no match for manuscript illumination like the coloured drawing of Caxton seeking inspiration from Ovid in a

---

[8] Piper, *English Face*, 27.   [9] Piper, *Image of the Poet*, 9–10.

[10] Ibid.; M. H. Spielmann, *The Portraits of Geoffrey Chaucer*, Chaucer Soc., 2nd ser., no. 31 (1900); Derek Pearsall, *The Life of Geoffrey Chaucer: A Critical Biography* (Oxford: Blackwell, 1992), appendix I.

[11] Corpus Christi Coll., Cambridge, MS 61, fo. 1ᵛ; see V. A. Kolve, *Chaucer and the Imagery of Narrative: The First Five Canterbury Tales* (London: Arnold, 1984), 377 n. 8.

[12] BL MS Lansdowne 851, fo. 2ʳ; Bodl. Libr. MS Bodl. 686, fo. 1a, illus. in Pearsall, *Chaucer*, pls 11, 12.

[13] But see ibid. 295–6.   [14] Ibid. 387, appendix I n. 6, pp. 343–4.

[15] Bodl. Libr., MS Bodl., 294 fo. 9; Bodl. 902, fo. 8. See J. A. W. Bennett (ed.), *Selections from John Gower* (Oxford: Clarendon Press, 1968), p. xxii; Gereth M. Spriggs, 'Unnoticed Bodleian Manuscripts, Illuminated by Herman Scheere and his School', *Bodleian Library Record*, 7 (1964), 193–203.

Magdalene manuscript of his *Metamorphoses* translation.[16] A woodcut of John Skelton appearing in *Certayn Bokes compiled by Mayster Skelton Poet Laureate* (*c.*1545), is captioned 'Skelton Poet', but probably without any attempt at a recognizable likeness. Skelton's profession is identified by a bookstand, books, and a laurel wreath: the portrait is generic.[17]

Renaissance medals achieved more convincing likenesses, at least after Pisanello, the first true Renaissance medallist.[18] With medals, the influence of antiquity was direct: many artists and *virtuosi*, from Petrarch on, collected Roman coins and medals.[19] Medals of poets and Italian humanists were avidly acquired: Dante, Boccaccio, Bembo, Ariosto, Ficino, Pico della Mirandola, Aretino, Pontano, and Pierio Valeriano. The vogue was consciously classicizing, extending as it did to Aristotle, Homer, and other ancient authors.[20] Northern humanists too had their medals, some cast by Quentin Massys the brilliant Antwerp medallist. His medal of Erasmus specifically claimed to be *ad vivam*, 'from the life'.[21] And Erasmus himself collected and exchanged medals, distributing copies as gifts: he preferred his own likeness by Massys to that by Dürer. Fewer medals were struck in Britain; but Nicholas Hilliard was active, and his James I was the portrait of a writer as well as a king.

From medals, portraiture carried over to frontispieces, where the image was often now printed within a circular frame.[22] It was again the Antwerp school that introduced, from about 1600, copper-engraved portraits.[23] Despite the difficulty of coordinating them with wooden type, a taste for these developed, and was catered to by many books of portraits.[24] Engraved

[16] Reproduced as frontispiece to *Selections from William Caxton*, ed. N. F. Blake (Oxford: Clarendon Press, 1973), p. xvi.

[17] See Piper, *Image of the Poet*, 8–9, 202, and fig. 7.

[18] See John Pope-Hennessy, *The Portrait in the Renaissance* (London: Phaidon Press; New York: Bollingen Series, 1966), 89.

[19] See Stephen K. Scher (ed.), *The Currency of Fame: Portrait Medals of the Renaissance* (New York: Abrams and the Frick Collection, 1994), 16.

[20] Hill and Pollard, 299, 300, 301, 386; Scher, *Fame*, 173; Hill and Pollard, 339, 268, 277, 475, 484a, Scher, *Fame*, 181; Hill and Pollard, 106, 507, 298, 399.

[21] Ibid. 629a; Pope-Hennessy, *The Portrait*, 92, 99; Scher, *Fame*, 249, 361.

[22] Piper, *Image of the Poet*, 20.   [23] Ibid. 20.

[24] Some are listed in Lucien Febvre and Henri-Jean Martin, *The Coming of the Book: The Impact of Printing 1450–1800*, trans. David Gerard (London: Verso, 1976), 101.

author portraits soon became usual for frontispieces and title pages. Johnson's *Catalogue*, to look no further, includes portraits of Moses, Hesiod, Juvenal, Ambroise Paré, and the divines Preston and Abbott. Modern authors include Samuel Daniel, John Taylor the Water Poet, Robert Burton (as Democritus Junior), Thomas More, Richard Brathwait, John Gerard, and James Howell (shown among busts of his ancient models).[25]

What if portraits of both author and translator were to be accommodated? Here the usual practice was to put the author portrait in the upper register, the translator in the lower. So Giovanni Paolo Lomazzo's portrait is above that of R. Haydock, Xenophon's above Philemon Holland's, Homer's above Chapman's, and Ariosto's above Harington's.[26] Classical authors tended to appear as busts, moderns as portraits. But there were exceptions, as when a modern poet such as Herrick identified himself as the avatar of an ancient. Or the printer might advertise himself by a portrait—a practice commoner on the Continent than in England.[27]

Medallion portraits could be framed by a single line or by several. Sir Thomas Wyatt's classicizing portrait from a Holbein original has no fewer than six concentric circles. This woodcut, first published in John Leland's *Naeniae in mortem Thomae Viati* (1542), shows the poet in loose, vaguely Roman costume.[28] Later, author portraits were regularly located on the title page, where medallion layouts, appropriating antique forms, became common.

Printers' devices inscribed on shields, as we shall see, expressed obvious social pretension. More subtle, perhaps, were inscriptions on cartouches. Considered as an architectural ornament in the form of a scroll (*OED* 2 b), or a paper tablet for inscription (*OED* 2 c), the cartouche seems innocent. Even in the form of an oval escutcheon (*OED* 3), its heraldic associations may appear harmlessly ecclesiastical. But the cartouche had other, distinctly secular, cultural associations. Card or leather cartouches generally had curled

---

[25] Johnson, *Catalogue*: Moses, Hollar 16; Hesiod, Marshall 28; Virgil, Marshall 113; Juvenal, Rawlins 8, Paraeus, Cecill 22; Preston 35; Abbott, Marshall 16; Daniel, Cockson 2; Taylor, Cockson 5; Burton, Le Blon 1; More, Marshall 55; Brathwait, Marshall 48; Gerard, Payne 9; Howell, Marshall 94.

[26] Johnson, *Catalogue*, Haydock 1, Hole 5, Marshall 8, Hole 1.

[27] See Hugh William Davies, *Devices of the Early Printers 1457–1560* (London: Grafton, 1935), 178 and ch. 10 *passim*.

[28] Reproduced in Piper, *Image of the Poet*, 11, 13, 203 n. 12.

edges resembling strapwork, a decorative style that originated at the Fontainebleau court of François I, an invention of the decorative genius Rosso Fiorentino (1494–1540).[29]

The immense popularity throughout Europe of strapwork in frontispieces and festival architecture had much to do with the glamour of the French court. Strapwork probably suggested the well-worn leather accoutrements of equestrian chivalry with its aristocratic implications. In title pages, strapwork might have varying degrees of explicitness. The title page of the English translation of Serlio's *First Book of Architecture* (1611) has a strapwork border that exploits every possible (and some impossible) convolutions. This popular block was used in Antwerp, Basle, and London.[30] In the title page of Samuel Daniel's *Works* (1602) the upper cartouche framing the royal arms and the motto SEM-PER EADEM is relatively subdued; but the lower, framing the imprint, is positively rococo in its intricacy.[31] In the same poet's *The Civil Wars* (1609), Hole has reworked the title page of Camden's *Britannia* (1607), replacing the map with Daniel's portrait.[32] The title—*The Civile Wares* [...] *Corrected and Continued by Samuel Daniel one of the Gromes of hir Maiesties Most Honourable Privie Chamber*—is framed by a strapwork cartouche which partially also encloses an oval portrait of the author, with a prominent elbow asserting his rank.[33] A separate cartouche, this time of acanthus, frames the imprint.

Leah Marcus suggests that 'there appears, in England at least, to have been considerable resistance until fairly late to the use of printed images of living poets.'[34] The validity of this depends heavily on what is considered 'fairly late'. Marcus assumes that living poets were not thought to rate portraits 'before the 1630s and 1640s'. But exceptions throng to mind: John Heywood (1556),

---

[29] See Fiorentino Rosso, *Drawings, Prints, and Decorative Arts*, ed. Eugene A. Carroll (Washington: National Gallery of Art, 1987), 71, figs 11–15 *et passim*; Margery Corbett, 'The Cartouche in English Engraving', *Motif*, 10, ed. Ruari McLean (London: Shenval, 1962), ch. 5.

[30] Reproduced in Alexander Nesbitt (ed.), *200 Decorative Title-Pages* (New York: Dover, 1964), pl. 87.

[31] Dated 1601 in some copies. Illus. in ibid., pl. 78.

[32] Johnson, *Catalogue*, 7; Cockson 2; Hole 2.

[33] See Joaneath Ann Spicer, 'The Renaissance Elbow', in Jan Bremmer and Herman Roodenburg (eds), *A Cultural History of Gesture* (Oxford: Polity; Ithaca, NY: Cornell University Press, 1992), 84–128.

[34] Leah S. Marcus, *Unediting the Renaissance: Shakespeare, Marlowe, Milton*, rev. edn (London: Routledge, 1996), 199.

Gascoigne (1576), Harington (1590), Sylvester (1614–15), James I (1616), Chapman (1616), Drummond (1616), Drayton (1619), and Cowley (1633). Marcus's argument from later insertion of portraits in Jonson's *Works* (1616) is double-edged, since it implies a portrait was expected. But her distinction between portraits of living and of dead poets is amply justified. It was customary to publish collected works just after a poet's death, so that the number of portrait frontispieces of recently dead poets is striking: Wyatt, Donne, and Herbert, for example.

The case of Milton is of special interest. Leah Marcus finds politics in William Marshall's portrait frontispiece before Milton's 1645 *Poems*. The Royalist Marshall, she thinks, portrayed Milton as an elderly cretin, and Milton took his revenge in a Greek epigraph below the portrait. Unable to read Greek, Marshall laboriously engraved the satiric verses about his own lack of skill. There may be something in this. Marshall was not a major artist by continental standards. But among English engravers he was one of those most often commissioned: he could hardly be called incompetent. Then again, perhaps the portrait was not a bad likeness. In any case, there was a long tradition of deriding portraitists. It goes back to Leonidas of Alexandria satirizing Diodorus, and Lucillius satirizing Menestratus and Eutychus (*Greek Anthology*, xi. 213–15). More recently, George Wither in 'Preposition to this Frontispiece' before his *Emblemes* (1635) had at first complained that William Marshall had failed to follow his brief:

> Our AUTHOR, to the *Graver* did commend
> A plaine Invention; that it might be wrought,
> According as his Fancie had forethought.
> Insteed thereof, the *Workeman* brought to light,
> What, here, you see: therein, mistaking quite
> The true *Designe* [...][35]

It was doubtless all part of the *Paragone* or contest of the arts. *Disegno* was supposed to be superior to physical realization. Wither designed the invention; but Marshall, 'the Workeman', mistook 'the true *Designe*'.

---

[35] Private information from the late Robert M. Cummings.

Printers' Devices

Many early modern printers used personal devices much like those of aristocrats and great merchants. The device resembled the modern logo in that it identified the printer and advertised his abilities by its witty economy in conveying appropriate associations.[1] Among the earliest printers' devices were trademarks, often the monograph or initials of the printer, as with I.H. (Jean Huvin of Rouen?) perhaps as early as 1496.[2]

There were many other sorts of device. Simplest and earliest (but long persisting) were representations of the sign or address of the printer's place of business. (Before numerical addresses, buildings were identified by pictorial

---

[1] For a bibliographical definition, see R. B. McKerrow, *Printers' and Publishers' Devices in England and Scotland 1485–1640* (1913; Oxford: Oxford University Press for the Bibliographical Society, 1949), pp. xii–xiii.
[2] Ibid., no. 8.

signboards.) The printer Thomas Berthelet used a device featuring Lucretia simply because he traded at a shop with that sign.[3] Similarly, the colophon of Tottel's *Songs and Sonnets* (1557, Q1) reads 'Imprinted at London in flete strete within temple barre, at the sygne of the hand and starre, by Richard Tottel the fift day of June An. 1557'. The immigrant binder and bookseller John Reynes traded at the sign of St George in St Paul's Churchyard near Cheap Gate, and R. Copeland and W. Copland at the sign of the Rose Garland in Fleet Street. Later, such information tended to appear on the title page. This type of device is naturally of particular interest to students of old signage.

Another type of device, the rebus, was especially significant for the history of the title page. The rebus expressed a proper name by substituting an associated common noun: a windmill, for example, might stand for *Miller* or for *Moulin*.[4] Or the rebus might play, like a syllabic anagram, on the several syllables of a name, as in *Hay–rye–sun* for *Harrison*.[5] The York printer Ursyn Mylner adopted the device of a bear (Latin *ursus, ursa*) and a mill.[6] Such devices have come to seem far-fetched. Richard Jugge used the rebus of a nightingale in a thorn, on the strength of *jug* being an imitative representation of the nightingale's call (*OED* sb.[3]). Jonson made fun of rebus devices (by then out of fashion) in *The Alchemist* (1610), where Subtle explains the device he has made for Abel Drugger:

> He first shall have a bell, that's 'A-bel'
> And by it standing one whose name is Dee,
> In a rug gown; there's 'D' and 'rug', that's 'Drug'.
> And right anenst [opposite] him a dog snarling 'Er';
> There's 'Drugger', 'Abel Drugger'. That's his sign.
>
> (2. 6. 19–23)

According to a commendatory letter before Paolo Giovio's *Discourse of Rare Inventions, Called* Imprese (1585), printers competed with one another in devising ingenious devices:

---

[3] Ibid., no. 80.   [4] Ibid., no. 22.

[5] Ibid., no. 143; see William Camden, *Remains Concerning Britain* (1605), ed. R. D. Dunn (Toronto: University of Toronto Press, 1984), 139–41.

[6] McKerrow, *Printers' and Publishers' Devices*, nos 38, 39, 88, 95.

Have [our printers] not [...] been at emulation for ingenious *Deuises*. [Stephanus] glorieth in his tree, and moderateth those [...] that love to mount by loftie witts [...] with this Posie: *Noli altum sapere* 'Be not proud'. Plantin beareth a compasse in a hande stretched out of the cloudes which measureth all, *Constantia & labore* [...] I will forget all artificers, who commonly buy such inventions at second hand.[7]

Printers invented or commissioned devices to display their powers of *disegno* and show themselves above the level of ordinary 'artificers'.

Printers' devices could be seen as laying claim to superior social status. They closely resembled chivalric *imprese*, which also relied on the art of the rebus and similarly incorporated allusive mottos. Indeed, Francis Thynne, Lancaster Herald, advised heralds 'to prohibit any merchant or any other to put their names, marks or devices in escutcheons on shields which belong and only appertain to gentlemen bearing arms and to none other'.[8] Despite this, many early title pages sported the printer's mark on a shield or cartouche, accompanied by a motto-like inscription. As Hugh William Davies puts it, the 'printer's device grew from the simple shield to the elaborate design complete with crest, supporters, motto, etc.'.[9] The mark of the printer Lawrence Andrewe (1527–30), for example, appears on a shield within a frame. And the monogram of J. Skot is on a shield suspended from a tree and flanked by two griffin supporters.[10]

Some title pages had blank shields for a customer to inscribe his own arms or monogram—or as if the printer anticipated his mark would soon be recognized heraldically.[11] Not that the arms on title pages were all merely wishful. The printer Richard Pynson had a real coat of arms.[12] And some other printers, such as William Marshall, used the arms of a more exalted branch of their family, or their patron, or some institution they belonged to. John Scolar used

---

[7] Paolo Giovio, *A Discourse of Rare Inventions, Called* Imprese, trans. Samuel Daniel (London, 1585); see Corbett and Lightbown, 15.

[8] Hugh William Davies, *Devices of the Early Printers 1457–1560* (London: Grafton, 1935), 26.

[9] Ibid. 96.

[10] Imitating the device of Denis Roce (Rosse), a French bookseller; see McKerrow, *Printers' and Publishers' Devices*, nos 74, 75.

[11] e.g. ibid., no. 134 (an empty cartouche); see Davies, *Devices of the Early Printers*, 26, 96.

[12] See J. W. Papworth, *An Alphabetic Dictionary of Coats of Arms* (London: Richards, 1874), 807.

the arms of the University of Oxford, and Rowland Hall, who had worked at Geneva from 1559 to 1560, continued to use its arms three years later.[13]

As Clarencieux King of Arms 1589–1623, William Camden had little liking for what he thought were groundless pretentions. In his essay 'Rebus, or Name-devises' he mocks those who lacked wit 'to express their conceit [invention] in speech, [but] did use to depaint it out (as it were) in pictures, which they called *Rebus*, by a Latine name well fitting their devise'. In Camden's view the rebus had a French origin.[14] But

they were so well entertained here (although they were most ridiculous) by all degrees, by the learned and unlearned, that he was nobody that coulde not hammer out of his name an invention by this witcraft, and picture it acccordingly: whereupon who did not busie his braine to hammer his devise out of this forge.[15]

In Camden's view, it was no accident that printers' devices resembled chivalric *imprese*.

Even when Camden admired a particular commoner using such a rebus, he contrived to suggest that doing so was beneath (or above) him. So 'Morton Archbishop of Canterbury, a man of great wisedome, and borne to the universall good of this realme, was content to use *Mor* upon a Tunne; and sometime a Mulbery tree called *Morus* in Latine out of a Tunne'.[16] At the same time, the great antiquity of the rebus was undeniable; which gave Camden pause. After explaining several devices, he added: 'In parte to excuse them yet, some of the greatest Romans were a little blasted with this foolerie, if you so censure it.'[17] He instanced the elephant on Julius Caesar's coins; which was chosen because (as Joseph Addison would later explain) 'the Word *Caesar* signifying an Elephant in the Punick language'.[18]

Camden amused himself at the expense of commoners such as John Morton or Thomas Chaundler (Warden of New College) who appropriated quasi-heraldic *imprese*; but he can hardly have felt the same about the learned

[13] McKerrow, *Printers' and Publishers' Devices*, nos 87, 143, 136.
[14] With good reason: see Jean Céard and Jean-Claude Margolin, *Rébus de la Renaissance: Des images qui parlent*, 2 vols (Paris: Maisonneuve and Larose, 1986).
[15] Camden, *Remains*, 139.   [16] Ibid. 141.   [17] Ibid.
[18] Joseph Addison, *The Spectator*, 59 (8 May 1711), 250.

continental scholar-printers. After all, the compasses of Plantin and the dolphin and anchor of Aldus Manutius were rebuses too. And the dolphin and anchor had antiquity enough: in AD 80 they appeared on an *aureus* of the emperor Titus, associated with the motto *festina lente, festina tarde,* or *speude brodeos* ('the more haste the less speed').[19]

As for the Estiennes themselves, they belonged to the printing aristocracy of Paris: Robert's father was an eminent academic publisher and bookseller.[20] And Robert was an earnest reformer, engaged in vast editing projects, including a new text of the Vulgate (1527) and a multi-volume Latin thesaurus (1543). From 1527 he adopted as his device the familiar olive tree with a broken branch (Fig. 8). The inscription *noli altum sapere* quotes Romans 11: 20, 'don't become proud, but stand in awe'. One might assume the olive tree to be the sign of his printing-house; but there is no evidence of its being an address. It is fully explained by the Pauline context, where the tree figures Israel (the Church or the Body of Christ) and the dead branch the unbelievers. Branches grafted in, however, are Gentiles belonging through faith to the tree of life (11: 19–24). Paul's metaphor of grafting was a key text in Reformation controversy,[21] so that Robert's device amounted to a reformist manifesto. Not surprisingly, he ran into trouble with the conservative theologians of Paris. Faced with charges of heresy, he found it best to leave for Calvinist Geneva.

Estienne's device, almost as much emblem as *impresa*, was full of allusive implications. In this, it had a strong influence on English printers.[22] This shows in the familiar device of Richard Grafton, printer to the king. Grafton's device is a rebus: it shows a *graft* growing through the bunghole of a barrel or *tun* (Fig. 9). The tun resembles those that books were packed in for transport, and is aptly inscribed with Grafton's trademark. A banderole bears as motto the biblical text *Suscipite incitum verbum*, 'Receive with meekness the [engrafted]

---

[19] Suetonius, *Div. Aug.* 2.25.4; see Alastair Fowler, 'The Emblem as a Literary Genre', in Michael Bath and Daniel Russell (eds), *Deviceful Settings* (New York: AMS, 1999), 2–3, 6.

[20] See Elizabeth Armstrong, *Robert Estienne: Royal Printer* (Cambridge: Cambridge University Press, 1954), p. xviii.

[21] e.g. Jean Calvin, *Institutes* 3.24.6; see Euan Cameron, *The European Reformation* (Oxford: Clarendon Press, 1991), 176.

[22] See McKerrow, *Printers, and Publishers' Devices*, p. xxv. The olive device was used by J. Wolfe, ibid., no. 310.

Fig. 8. Robert Estienne's device, *Biblia sacra* (Paris, 1532). Gibson 123, Title Page. Courtesy of the Bodleian Libraries, The University of Oxford.

Fig. 9. Richard Grafton's rebus, *Iniunctions* (1547). Reproduced by kind permission of the Syndics of Cambridge University Library.

word' (James 1: 21).[23] Grafton's device, like Estienne's, depends on the Pauline metaphor of grafting, and takes up a Reformist stance. Yet it also reflects unmistakable social ambition. In the title page of *The Chronicle of Jhon Hardyng* (1543), Grafton's mark appears on a shield with putti acting as supporters.[24]

But the ideology of the device should not be overemphasized. In the context of printing with wooden types and woodcuts, metaphors of trees were hard to avoid. Many title pages attempted wit of a similar kind. They would pun on 'tree', or 'family tree', or place the printer's initials on a shield suspended from a tree. Emblems too exploited arboreal associations.[25]

In André Favyn's *The Theater of Honour and Knight-Hood* [...] *The First Institution of Armes* [...] (1623), tradesmen not noble are said to be allowed only 'Markes or notes of those Trades and Professions which they used: as a tailor to have his sheares, a cutler a knife [...] a mason his trowel, and the compasse or squire, and so of other'.[26] One might expect printers to have used images of the printing press in their devices—as did several continental printers, for example Th. De Borne Deventer (c.1518), Jodocus Badius (1520), and Jean Roigny (1539).[27] But, in Britain, images of printing were rare: perhaps because printing there had not yet achieved comparable social status. One example, however, is the title page of Robert Pont, *De sabbaticorum annorum periodis chronologica digestio*, printed by G. Jones, which shows two printers at work with lighted candles fixed on their heads.[28]

Sometimes, when a commission was too large for the resources of a single printing-house, collaboration was called for. Then the title page might have to accommodate several devices. The title page of a 1574 *Liber precum publicarum*, printed by Thomas Vautrollier and Francis Flower's assignees, has no fewer than six devices, arranged in the niches of a pegme or framework, with the royal arms above and the Stationers' below (Fig. 10).[29] All six devices are

[23] By error the quotation is given as *suscipite incitum verbum*. For the rebus, see McKerrow, *Printers' and Publishers' Devices*, nos 114, 88, 95, etc.

[24] Ibid., no. 92; cf. nos 88, 95, 104, 110, 114, 122. For Grafton's biography, see C. J. Sisson, 'Grafton and the London Grey Friars', *The Library*, 4th ser., 11 (1931), 121–49.

[25] See Fowler, 'The Emblem', 15, 19–20 n. 70.

[26] *Theatre d'Honneur et de chevalerie* (Paris, 1620), trans. A.M. (perhaps Anthony Munday) (London: [Jaggard], 1623). Davies, *Devices of the Early Printers*, 26.

[27] See ibid., ch. 10, esp. p. 162 and fig. 247. See Falconer Madan, 'Early Representations of the Printing-Press', *Bibliographica*, 1 (1895), 223–48, 494–504, esp. 226–9, 235.

[28] McKerrow, *Printers' and Publishers' Devices*, no. 389.   [29] Ibid., no. 169.

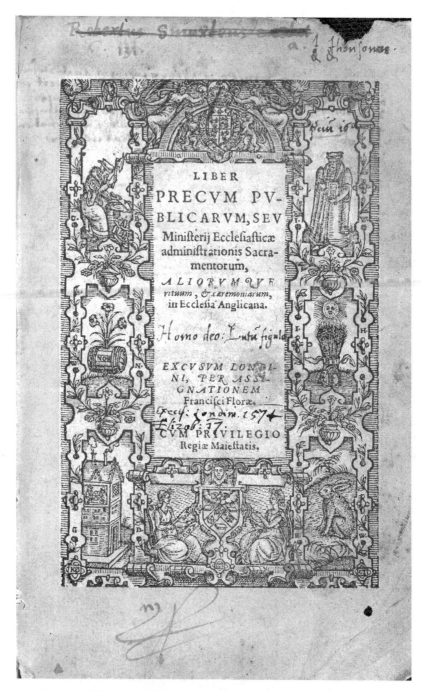

Fig. 10. Multiple devices, *Liber precum publicarum* (1574). Vet. A3. E. 727. Courtesy of the Bodleian Libraries, The University of Oxford.

rebuses: a man *barking* logs (Christopher Barker); men dicing in a *garret* and casting a *deuce* (Garret Dewes); a gowned man or *wight* carrying the book *scientia* ('knowledge') with the initials I.W. (John Wight) and the motto 'welcome the wight that bringeth such light'; *hare*, *rye*, and *sun* for Harrison; NOR and *tun* for W. Norton; and a hare, implying *Wat* (type name for a hare) for R. Watkins.[30]

The images in printers' devices—and frontispieces generally—were seldom unique to one edition. Woodcuts and engravings were expensive, and consequently were often reused, sometimes with very different applications. A cut of St George energetically transfixing a dragon with his lance may be familiar from its appearance between books 1 and 2 of *The Faerie Queene* (1590). But, four years earlier, it had been used as a frontispiece in G.G.'s (Gilbert Gifford's?) news pamphlet *A Briefe Discoverie of Doctor Allens Seditious Drifts* [...] *Concerning the Yielding up of the Towne of Deventer* [...] (1588). The cut seems to have belonged to J. Wolfe, who used it eight times, from 1588 to 1592, before passing it to R. Field.[31]

---

[30] Cf. McKerrow, *Printers' and Publishers' Devices*, no. 190; Camden, *Remains*, 141; McKerrow, *Printers' and Publishers' Devices*, no. 205; ibid., no. 143, Camden, *Remains*, 141; McKerrow, *Printers' and Publishers' Devices*, nos 174, 175; ibid., no. 174; Shakespeare, *Venus and Adonis*, line 697.

[31] See Luborsky and Ingram, 311.

Emblems

The rebus and the device (Italian *impresa*; Latin *symbolum*) became fashionable in France from the fourteenth century and in Italy from the fifteenth. The *impresa*—literally 'undertaking, enterprise'—expressed a personal ideal or aspiration, and as such was capable of brilliantly varied application. Whole books have been devoted to the *imprese* of Federico da Montefeltro, which formed the basis of rich decoration at his palace of Urbino. Even the sides of an inkpot carry the letters FEDE, playing on the name FEDERICO. Such devices could be so individual as to puzzle anyone not belonging to his in-group.

Devices were used everywhere: not only in tournaments, but as house and inn signs, hat badges, murals, painted ceilings—and title pages.[1] As we saw in

---

[1] e.g. the ceiling at Pinkie House: see Michael Bath, *Renaissance Decorative Painting in Scotland* (Edinburgh: National Museums of Scotland Publishing, 2003). On the forty-three emblems in Lady Drury's oratory at Hawstead Hall, see Norman K. Farmer, *Poets and the*

the previous chapter, such devices as Aldo Manuzio's FESTINA LENTE and Francesco Calvo's elephant had a history going back to antiquity. To some, devices were subjects for meditation. Their explanation or invention might call for the help of learned interpreters. For materials, the inventors turned to the natural world and to literature, especially classical mythology and Petrarchan love poetry. Coins and medals, too, offered abundant sources— besides being a direct physical link with the ancient world. The emblematist might also draw motifs from the romantic past of chivalry: dragons and woodwoses, heroes and exotic animals.

Soon there was a literature on devices, mostly continental. Rules were set out in such works as Paolo Giovio's *Dialogo dell'imprese* (1555) and Girolamo Ruscelli's *Le imprese illustri con espositioni* (1566). Occasionally, however, the authorities disagreed: Giovio ruled that human figures should never appear in devices; Ruscelli saw no reason to exclude them. Giovio's *Dialogo* went through several unillustrated editions before the fine Lyons 1559 edition by Guillaume Rouillé. In England the *Dialogo* was in part translated by Samuel Daniel as *A Discourse of* [...] *imprese* (1585);[2] Abraham Fraunce's *Insignium, armorum, emblematum, hieroglyphicorum, et symbolorum, quae ab Italis imprese nominantur, explicatio* (1588) made an independent contribution;[3] and William Scott (*c.*1571–*c.*1617) attempted a more popular survey in *The Model of Poesy*.[4]

Illustrations generally had to be specially commissioned from artists: Giovio's device invented for Girolamo Adorno was designed by Titian and embroidered by the Venetian Agnolo di Madonna. In England, Sir Henry Lee, Queen Elizabeth's champion, commissioned several allegorical programmes and *imprese* from the painter Marcus Gheeraerts.[5]

Visual Arts in Renaissance England (Austin, TX: University of Texas Press, 1984), 77–105; H. L. Meakin, *The Painted Closet of Lady Ann Bacon Drury* (Farnham: Ashgate, 2013).

[2] Samuel Daniel, *The Worthy Tract of Paulus Jovius, Contayning A Discourse of Rare Inventions, Both Militarie and Amorous Called* Imprese (London: Hardpress, n.d.).

[3] See Abraham Fraunce, *Symbolicae philosophiae liber quartus et ultimus*, ed. John Manning, trans. Estelle Haan (New York: AMS, 1991).

[4] William Scott, *The Model of Poesy*, ed. Gavin Alexander (Cambridge: Cambridge University Press, 2013).

[5] See ibid., p. lxiv; Alan R. Young, *Tudor and Jacobean Tournaments* (London: George Philip, 1987), 140–3.

From the mid-sixteenth century, a new form, the emblem, arose on the continent. It developed out of the device, but was less individual, and potentially more accessible.[6] This is not to say it was more easily legible. Like the device, it had meanings deeper than those of its motto or its visual metaphor. These were allusive, whether alluding to each other or to some abstract *tertium quid*. The close association of emblem and device is clear from Scott's conflating them: 'this is by *emblem* and more properly by that noble device of *impresa*.'[7] Emblems dominated the design of so many title pages and frontispieces that Corbett and Lightbown subtitled their study *The Emblematic Title-Page*.

If the emblem had a single inventor, it was Andrea Alciato (1492–1550). But Alciato's *Emblematum liber* (Augsburg, 1531) originally consisted of 'nude emblems'—that is, lemmas and epigrams only, without illustrations. The publisher, Heinrich Steyner, added the pictures. A good deal of evidence goes to suggest this was the usual practice: publishers needed to encourage sales of what was at first a learned, even esoteric, genre.

Eventually theorists began to distinguish the emblem from the device.[8] As Daniel (or 'N.W.') explained, *imprese* are individual and personal, whereas 'emblems are general conceiptes rather of moral matters than perticulare deliberations, rather to give credit to the wit, then to reveale the secrets of the minde'.[9] The emblemist Geoffrey Whitney wrote of emblems as concerned with three matters: 'three Kindes [...] Historical, Naturall, and Moral.' By far the most interesting early theorist was the seventeenth-century Claude-François Menestrier (1631–1705).[10]

Within this broad field of emblem, specialisms emerged. Joachim Camerarius' *Symbola* (Nuremberg, 1593) drew emblems from nature; Théodore de Beze's *Icones* (Geneva, 1580) assembled portraits of exemplary leaders; and Achille Bocchi's elegant *Symbolicarum quaestionum de universo* (Bologna, 1555) followed Alciato in concentrating on moral abstractions. Most emblematists

---

[6] Alastair Fowler, 'The Emblem as a Literary Genre', in Michael Bath and Daniel Russell (eds), *Deviceful Settings: The English Renaissance Emblem and its Contexts*, Selected Papers from the Third International Emblem Conference, Pittsburgh, 1993 (New York: AMS, 1999), 12.

[7] Scott, *Poesy*, 81 line 28.

[8] See Mario Praz, *Studies in Seventeenth-Century Imagery*, 2nd enlarged edn (Rome: Edizioni di Storia e Letteratura, 1964), ch. 1.

[9] Cf. Corbett and Lightbown, 17.

[10] For a survey of his works, see Praz, *Studies*, 421–4.

deliberately pursued difficulty, an aim that excluded the common reader—and enhanced the interpreter's role.

Illustrations, if present, were executed according to instructions from the author or publisher. Or, more cost-effectively, they might be taken over from other works.[11] Unusually, Otto van Veen, a humanist–artist of noble descent, produced his own illustrations for several emblem books, including one for the English market: *Amorum emblemata: Emblemes of Love with Verses in Latin, English, and Italian* (Antwerp, 1608). Henry Peacham, a courtier able to draw, presented Prince Henry with an illustrated manuscript of emblems, later published as *Minerva Britanna* (1612). And Mildmay Fane, Earl of Westmorland, put together a manuscript collection of his poems, with rough emblematic headpieces.[12] The collection of *Poems 1623–50*[13] has a title page showing the decorated title *Emblemata* with, immediately below, the representation of a horse.[14] Below this again, an eight-line epigram identifies the horse as *Bellerophontis equus*—that is, Pegasus, an emblem of poetic inspiration.[15]

Material for emblems was drawn, as we have seen, from ancient and medieval sources. Coins and medals were particularly important: in *The Compleat Gentleman* (1634) Henry Peacham asks:

Would you see the true and undoubted modells of their Temples, Alters, Deities, Columnes, Gates, Arches, Aquaeducts, Bridges, Sacrifices, Vessels, *Sellae Curules*, Ensignes and Standards, Navall and murall Crownes, Amphytheaters, Circi, Bathes, Chariots, Trophies, Ancilia, and a thousand things more [...][16]

Coins usually showed symbolic objects or exemplary historical figures, with allegories on the obverse. (The obverse of a coin of Severus Alexander, for

---

[11] See Corbett and Lightbown, 20.

[12] See Mildmay Fane, *The Poetry of Mildmay Fane: From the Fulbeck, Harvard and Westmorland Manuscripts*, ed. Tom Cain (Manchester: Manchester University Press, 2001), 6, 70–194, 379–403, 449–53.

[13] Cain's title for the Fulbeck Hall MS he designates MS 2.

[14] Fulbeck Hall MS 2, fo. 15ʳ. Cain prints the title but omits the paratext.

[15] Cf., e.g., A. I. I. Boissard, *Emblemata* (Frankfurt, 1596), emblem 49.

[16] Henry Peacham, *Peacham's Compleat Gentleman* (1634), ed. G. S. Gordon (Oxford: Clarendon Press, 1906), 123–4.

example, depicts Mars holding a reversed spear and an olive branch, with the inscription MARS PACIFERO.[17]) Together with the explanations of authorities—Guillaume Rouillé, Gabriello Simeoni, and especially the Lyons antiquary Guillaume du Choul[18]—coins sometimes offered ready-made symbols.

But literary sources were most useful of all: ancient and medieval mythographies such as Hyginus' *Fabulae* and *Poeticon Astronomicon*; Fulgentius' broadly allegorical *Mythologicon*; and, by far the most important, Ovid's *Metamorphoses*. The Renaissance reintegration of the ancient gods began in ambitious works such as Giovanni Boccaccio's in *Genealogia deorum gentilium* (?1350–75)[19] and Lilius Gregorius Gyraldus' *De deis gentium* (Basle, 1548), distinguishing hundreds of ancient divinities, their cults and representations. Such early surveys were digested in accessible and immensely influential handbooks: Vincenzo Cartari's *Le imagini colla spositione de i dei de gli antichi* (Venice, 1556); Natale Conti's *Mythologiae, sive explicationum fabularum libri decem* (Basle, 1568); and Cesare Ripa's *Iconologia* (Rome, 1593). A wide-ranging modern essay, Jean Seznec's *The Survival of the Pagan Gods* (1940, 1953), traces the disintegration of the pagan gods and their partial reintegration in Renaissance iconography.

Early theorists overemphasized the importance of Egyptian hieroglyphs—

concerning the arte of *Imprese* [...] it is knowne that it descended from the auncient Aegiptians [...] who devised meanes before Characters [letters] were founde out, to utter their conceiptes [ideas] by formes of Beastes, Starres, Hearbes [...] By a serpent pollicie. By an Olive peace. By a Gote lust[20]

---

[17] Luciano Cheles, *The Studiolo of Urbino: An Iconographical Investigation* (University Park, PA: Pennsylvania State University Press, 1986), 84–5.

[18] Guillaume du Choul, *Discours de la religion des anciens Romains* (Lyons, 1556); Guillaume Rouillé, *Promptuaire des médailles* (Lyons, 1553); Gabriele Simeoni, *Illustratione de gli epitaffi et medaglie antique* (Lyons, 1558). Modern authorities include Sir George Hill, *Corpus of Italian Medals of the Renaissance before Cellini*, 2 vols (1930); rev. and enlarged by Graham Pollard as *Renaissance Medals at the National Gallery of Art* (London: Phaidon Press for the Samuel H. Kress Foundation, 1967); Stephen K. Scher (ed.), *The Currency of Fame: Portrait Medals of the Renaissance* (New York: Abrams and the Frick Collection, 1994).

[19] Trans. by Jon Solomon as *Genealogy of the Pagan Gods*, I Tatti Renaissance Library (Cambridge, MA: Harvard University Press, 2011–), i.

[20] Samuel Daniel: see Corbett and Lightbown, 22.

—giving what now seems far too much attention to Horapollo's *Hieroglyphica*, rediscovered in 1419.[21] This led them to pursue the chimera of an original hieroglyphic language. Still, a positive result was an important syncretic work, Pierio Valeriano's *Hieroglyphica* (Basle, 1556). Pierio's idea of antiquity was broad enough to include biblical and patristic material. In England, this valuable compilation (later enlarged with valuable *Collectanea*) was well known to Abraham Fraunce—who refers to Pierio's 'great commentaries'— and was used as a school textbook.

Corbett and Lightbown's *The Comely Frontispiece* shows how often Renaissance title pages were emblematic, sharing an iconography once familiar. Things represented in a frontispiece generally had metaphorical purposes: they were drawn 'from the world, as from a volume wherein was written the wonders of nature'. Some still think of emblems as conveying simple, eloquent contents. Nicholas Hookes's *Amanda* (1653), for example, has an engraved frontispiece that shows four putti carrying a coffin inscribed TO AN UNKNOWN GODDESSE, while a fifth lights a taper from a flaming heart.[22] But it is now widely recognized that emblems more often allude to multiple texts and meanings in a complex way. In the title page of Jonson's *Works* (1616), for example, one of the figures flanking Tragi-Comedy is a satyr, the goatish rural god with his pan-pipes (Frontispiece 6; p. 114). This satyr appears in Alciato's Emblem 72, Luxuria; for *satyri nymphas semper amare solent*.[23] But the same satyr figures in Emblem 98 as Natura,[24] closer to the lofty cosmic abstraction appearing in the frontispiece to Sherburne's translation of Manilius' *Sphere*: *Naturae vniversitas* (Frontispiece 11; p. 156).

Older accounts of the emblem described it as divided into three parts: motto or lemma, picture, and epigram. But John Manning and others have shown emblem structure to be much more variable than this suggests. An emblem might consist of as many as six parts or as few as one or two (in the

[21] *The Hieroglyphics of Horapollo*, trans. and ed. George Boas (New York: Pantheon, 1950).

[22] *The Grolier Club's Catalogue of Original and Early Editions of Some of the Poetical and Prose Works of English Writers from Langland to Prior*, 4 vols in 1 (Holland Press, 1964), no. 462: *Amanda. A Sacrifice to an Unknown Goddesse, or, A Freewill Offering of a loving Heart to a Sweet-Heart* (1653).

[23] Andrea Alciati, *Emblemata cum commentariis* (Padua: Pietro Paolo Tozzi, 1621; facsimile edn, New York and London: Garland, 1976), 321.

[24] Ibid. 409–13.

case of a 'nude', or unillustrated, emblem).[25] The tripartite structure may simply have arisen as a standard page layout. The emblem motto or lemma (Greek, 'title, heading, argument, something taken for granted') developed from the device, but in a less individual direction. It could be a quotation (*Facilis descensus Averni*), or a phrase summing up the content (*Ficta religio*).[26]

When an emblem was illustrated, the picture need not have been intended by the emblematist himself. Woodblocks were often reused in different emblem books, or perhaps with quite different mottos and epigrams.[27] Again, the picture might contribute an additional metaphor, or merely illustrate the implied 'narrative'. As for the epigram, it might be expository, enlarging on the motto or explaining the picture. It might be *ekphrastic*, describing and enlivening the picture. Or else it might describe another, comparable work, throwing light on the first.[28]

When George Wither desiderated a title page 'that's emblematicall', how much did he imply? Did he mean that each title page feature should correspond to an emblem 'part'? Did he mean that the title was a sort of motto? The printer's device, as we have seen, was often a rebus. The epigraph could be seen as an emblem epigram. And the pictorial features might correspond to the *pictura*. After all, 'architectural' ornaments already had figurative meanings: an obelisk might symbolize Fame and a column Fortitude. Alternatively, as in Charles V's *plus ultra* device, columns signified limits.[29] As for *tableaux* of symbolic persons with attributes drawn from Ripa or Cartari, these obviously corresponded to abstractions like those of Alciato's emblems. Corbett and Lightbown trace various figures of *Religio*: a Calvinist *Religio* appears in Beza's *Icones* (1580), James I's vision of the Church in his *Workes* (1616),[30] and a comparable figure in Hollar's title page for the Marquess of Winchester's translation of Talon's *The Holy History* (1653).[31] One might add the more satiric *Ficta religio* of Alciato, pictured as a throned queen intoxicating her followers, or as the harlot of Revelation riding a seven-headed dragon.[32]

---

[25] See John Manning, *The Emblem* (London: Reaktion, 2002), 42.

[26] Ibid. 369 n. 49, 205.   [27] Ibid. 85 *et passim*.   [28] Ibid. 103–5.

[29] Ibid. 75; Corbett and Lightbown, 32. Cf., e.g., Johnson, *Catalogue*, Hole No. 14 (obelisk and columns); de Passe No. 2 (limit of aspiration).

[30] Corbett and Lightbown, 38.   [31] Johnson, *Catalogue*, Hollar No. 16.

[32] Andrea Alciati, *Emblematum libellus* (Venice: Aldus, 1546) and *Emblemata omnia* (Paris, 1583); see Manning, *The Emblem*, 277.

A compelling reason for treating some title pages as emblematic is their accompanying texts in the form of an explanatory epigram. Herbert Golzius' *Fasti magistratuum et triumphorum Romanorum* (Bruges, 1561) had its *Frontispicii Explanatio*; John Guillim's *Displaye of Heraldrie* (1610) had its 'Epigram'; Sir Walter Raleigh's *The History of the World* (1614) had Ben Jonson's 'The Minde of the Frontispiece to a Booke'; Michael Drayton's *Poly-Olbion* (1612) had 'Upon the *Frontispice*'; and John Bulwer's *Philocophus* (1648) had 'A Reflection of the sence and minde of the Frontispiece'.[33] Without additional explanation, apparently, pictorial title pages could seem obscure. Just as an explanatory epigram often formed part of an emblem, so an explicatory poem might accompany an emblematic frontispiece. The parts of a book's front matter may be thought of as corresponding to the parts of emblem, with pictorial frontispiece matching *pictura* and title matching lemma.

Picture and words in an emblem were said to be related as body and soul in a person. Giovio required that in an *impresa* 'there should be a just proportion and agreement between its "soul" and its "body", i.e., its motto and image'.[34] And William Scott considered that in emblems and *imprese* 'the artisan [artist] brings his portraiture [illustration] as the body, the poet the speech and word as the soul, neither being of use without the other'.[35] Emblem components were similarly interdependent: 'the body or picture [is] a lifeless carcase if it be not informed and actuated by the word as the spirit'.[36] Abraham Fraunce (fl. 1587–1633), one who thought deeply about the nature of the emblem, regarded its 'mind' as close to what we might call authorial intention.[37] Yet he wrote of 'the motto' as 'not the soul of the *impresa* but that single resemblance which occupies mid place between the peculiar nature of the object and the idea conceived within the mind'.[38] By a natural extension, it followed that the emblematic title page acted as the soul or meaning of the book that followed.[39]

---

[33] See Corbett and Lightbown, 19, 46–7, 130, 154, 212. For other examples, see Michael Saenger, *The Commodification of Textual Engagements in the English Renaissance* (Aldershot and Burlington, VT: Ashgate, 2006), 76–8. Add Crashaw's 'The frontispiece explained' accompanying Henry Isaacson's *Saturni ephemerides* (1633).

[34] Manning, *The Emblem*, 75.

[35] Scott, *Poesy*, 81 lines 28–31.　　[36] Ibid. 81 lines 31–3.

[37] See Fraunce, *Symbolicae philosophiae liber quartus et ultimus*, 5–7, 21.　　[38] Ibid. 37.

[39] See Daniel S. Russell, *The Emblem and Device in France* (Lexington, KY, 1985), 41, 43, and *passim*; Fowler, 'The Emblem as a Literary Genre', 18.

Chronograms

A chronogram is a string of words, in which some or all of the letters
function also as numerals forming a date. In Hebrew and Greek, many
letters are also numerals, and chronograms abound, occurring as early as
Euripides. In Latin, however, only M, D, C, L, X, V, and I are numerals, and
chronograms appear much later. In the title page of John Dee's *General and
Rare Memorials*, Greek numerals appear openly (Frontispiece 3; p. 86).

During the seventeenth century chronograms became fashionable, particularly in Jesuit circles. For a time they appeared everywhere, 'on old medals,
bells, church windows, tombstones, and the title-pages of books'.[1] With the
Enlightenment's fashion for transparent language, however, chronograms

---

[1] See Tony Augarde, *The Oxford Guide to Word Games* (Oxford: Oxford University Press,
1984), 93–5.

came to be disparaged: they were regarded, with anagrams and acrostics, as 'kinds of false Wit that vanished in the refined Ages of the World'.[2]

In overt chronograms, numeral letters were usually capitalized for ease of recognition. In his *Scribleriad* (1752) Richard Cambridge figures such uneven letters as irregular troops:

> Not thus the looser chronograms prepare,
> Careless their troops, undisciplined to war,
> With ranks irregular, confused, they stand,
> The chieftains mingling with the vulgar band.[3]

Chronograms continued to be common into the nineteenth century. James Hilton claimed to have gathered as many as 38,411 of them.[4] And one reviewer thought that 'chronograms are so much more foolish, so much more senseless, and so much easier to make and to guess that there is every reason to fear an outbreak of them before long'.[5] A long way from Robert Burton's view, when he compared finding chronograms to the difficult search for the philosopher's stone.[6] Easy, yet difficult: how are we to resolve the contradiction?

It proves to be a relatively simple matter of distinguishing two quite different sorts of chronogram. In the ordinary, overt sort, the numerical letters are obvious from being in a distinctive type, usually large capitals. Such chronograms require minimal skill, whether of invention or discovery. Consequently, they have little interest or value. In the other sort—the hidden or embedded chronogram—the numeral letters are not overtly distinguished. Readers must discover them by applying rules of availability known to the initiated. These rules are quite different from those of overt, vulgar chronograms. Being harder to construct and discover, the covert chronogram was formerly more highly valued.

---

[2] Joseph Addison, in *The Spectator*, 60 (9 May 1711); ed. Donald F. Bond, 5 vols (Oxford: Clarendon Press, 1965), i. 253; cf. i. 256, 265.

[3] Augarde, *Word Games*, 92; Isaac Disraeli, *Curiosities of Literature*, 3 vols, rev. edn (London: Warne, 1881), i. 296.

[4] James Hilton, *Chronograms Continued and Concluded* [...] *A Supplement* (London: Elliot Stock, 1885).

[5] Augarde, *Word Games*, 95–6.

[6] Robert Burton, *The Anatomy of Melancholy*, ed. J. B. Bamborough, Thomas C. Faulkner, et al., 6 vols (Oxford: Clarendon Press, 1989–2000), 2.2.4.1.

In covert chronograms, any surplus of unused numeral letters (M, D, C, L, X, or V) is not considered a defect: it is merely a consequence of some letters being available, others not. The rules for availability are much like those for concealed anagrams. To be available, numeral letters or groups of letters must be in acrostic positions—that is, must come at the beginning or end of a word, or word stem. But this rule is relaxed for *I*, presumably because in English this letter seldom ends a word. Thus, *I* is considered available in any position. The substitutions *C for K*, *X for S*, and *V for U* are allowed, as with anagrams.[7]

Hidden chronograms were quite often located in epigraphs, where the small room for manœuvre makes them least expected. For example, the title page of George Herbert's *The Temple* has an epigraph from the Book of Common Prayer (Ps 29: 8 in Coverdale's translation): IN HIS TEMPLE DOTH EVERY MAN SPEAK OF HIS HONOUR. Here, the medial M of TEMPLE is not available, but the initial M of MAN is available, and so is the initial D of DOTH and the terminal K of SPEAK, by substitution counted as C. Similarly, the terminal S's of HIS...HIS and the initial S of SPEAK by substitution yield three X's. And finally there are three I's. So we arrive at the date MDCXXXIII. In short, a chronogram of 1633, the year of publication.

It must often have tested a poet's skill to choose for the epigraph an apposite quotation with the requisite letters in available positions. Sometimes a few unimportant words might be replaced in order to arrive at the desired numeral letters. Such 'errors' or inelegances now may serve as clues to the searching scholar. In Richard Crashaw's *The Delights of the Muses* (1646), for example, the title page has an epigraph from Martial's *Epigram* 8.3.12, in which the wording has been adapted slightly, to arrive at DIC MIHI QUID MELIUS DESIDIOSUS AGAS ('Tell me, what better thing when idle might you do'). With this adjustment, the numeral letters MDCXXXXVI yield the publication date, 1646.

The thought underlying a Renaissance chronogram is expressed with unusual fullness in 'On the Frontispiece of Isaacsons Chronologie explained', a thirty-eight-line poem once attributed to Crashaw.[8]

---

[7] See William Camden, *Remains Concerning Britain*, ed. R. D. Dunn (Toronto: University of Toronto Press, 1984), 142.

[8] More probably the author is Edward Rainbow, later Bishop of Carlisle; see Richard Crashaw, *The Poems*, ed. L. C. Martin (Oxford: Clarendon Press, 1927), 410–11, 463.

If with distinctive Eye, and Mind, you looke
Upon the *Front*, you see more than one Booke.
Creation is *Gods Booke*, wherein he writ.
Each Creature is a Letter filling it.
History is *Creations* Booke; which showes
To what effects the *Series* of it goes.
Chronologie's the Booke of *Historie*, and beares
The just account of *Dayes, Moneths*, and *Yeares*.
But *Resurrection*, in a Later Presse,
And *New Edition*, is the summe of these.
....
The *Columnes* both are crown'd with either *Sphere*.
To show *Chronology* and *History* beare
No other *Culmen*; then the double Art
Astronomy, Geography, impart.

(Lines 1–10, 35–8)

In such discourse, every date had significance in the divine scheme of chronology. As the italicized words make almost explicit, creation was conceived as God's book, with individual creatures as letters in its text; history was creation's book; and chronology was history's book. In the new edition of creation's book, all the individual parts of time may be comprehended.

Compartments

Many early title pages have two distinct aims: to advertise the contents that follow, and to facilitate memorizing them. The two combine in the memorial title pages of the seventeenth century. These summarize the contents, sometimes explicitly analysing them, sometimes supplying memorable images or vignettes.

Lists of contents pre-dated print. In some manuscript books, indeed, these were the only front matter.[1] A fine example, used by Margaret Smith as her own frontispiece, is a Florentine manuscript of Boethius' *Opera* (*c*.1485).[2] Here, a central roundel frames the title, while subsidiary roundels frame the contents

---

[1] See Margaret Smith, *The Title-Page: Its Early Development 1460–1510* (British Library and Oak Knoll Press, 2000), 13, 41, 48, 99–101, 142.

[2] Ibid., 23–4: BL MS Landsdowne 842a, fo. 1ᵛ.

or part titles (for example, BOETH DE TRINITATE LIBRI II). Early printed examples could be even simpler, as in the list of contents, laid out in a half-diamond pattern, that serves as the title page of Cicero's *Orator* (Venice, 1492).[3] A more elaborate example, again Venetian, is Cicero's *Epistolae ad familiares* (1494) with woodcut author portraits of Cicero and his four commentators (three named) above a list of contents headed *Hoc in volumine haec continentur*.[4] The contents list continued as a common feature of title pages well into the seventeenth century—as in Holcroft's translation of Procopius' *History of Justinian*, published by Moseley in 1653.[5]

The Procopius title page is pictorial to the extent of displaying the title on a cloth. Elsewhere the contents list itself was presented pictorially. Already in a Venice *Biblia* of 1493 a double-page spread begins Genesis with vignettes of the six days of Creation.[6] And in the frontispiece of Harington's *Orlando furioso* (1591) vignettes on the column bases display the contents: love and war. But contents lists found more obvious pictorial realizations when title pages came to be divided into compartments. Probably more than a fifth of Johnson's facsimile title pages are divided, with each compartment illustrating a topic of the book.

A pace-setter in this was Robert Burton's *Anatomy of Melancholy*. From the 1628 edition onwards, the frontispiece has ten compartments. In 1632 'The Argument of the Frontispiece' explains the relevance of each compartment's 'symbol'. The top left compartment or 'square', for example, is explained as follows:

> To th' left a Landskip of Jealousye,
> Presents it selfe unto thine eye.
> A Kingfisher, a Swan, an Herne,
> Two fighting Cockes you may decerne,
> Two roareing Bulles each other high,
> To assault concerning Venery.

---

[3] Ibid., figs 6.3, 6.5. Cf. Herodotus, *Historiae* (Venice, 1494), listing nine part titles after the main title.

[4] Smith, *Title-Page*, 98, fig. 6.4.

[5] Illus. Johnson, *Catalogue*, Thomas Cross, No. 15.

[6] Illus. Smith, *Title-Page*, 136–7.

> Symbols are these, I say no more,
> Conceave the rest by that's afore.[7]

The kingfisher, for example, symbolized married love or uxoriousness; the swan, jealousy; the heron, suspicion.

During the 1620s and 1630s, compartmented title pages became fashionable: a great many of the familiar title pages in Johnson's *Catalogue* are of this type.[8] The best-known example of all, however, is surely Hobbes's *Leviathan* title page of 1651 (Frontispiece 9; p. 142).

Topics to be memorized were often arranged in 'decades' or sets of ten, as in the *Anatomy of Melancholy* title page. This was to assist the memory. As Hugh Platte explains in *The Jewell House of Art and Nature*:

> You must make choice of some large edifice or building [...] so familiar unto you, as that everie part of each of them may present it selfe readily unto the eyes of your minde when you call for them. In everie of these roomes you must place ten severall subjects [...] Your subjectes must consist of Decades.
>
> (*The Jewel House* (1594), 81–5)

Memorizing by decades was once a standard practice. In Ben Jonson's first play, for example, Francisco says:

> I will be silent, yet that I may serve
> But as a *Decade* in the art of memory
> To put you still in mind of your owne vertues
> (When your too serious thoughts make you too sad)
> Accept me for your servant honor'd Lady.
>
> (*The Case is Altered*, 2. 4. 39–44)

---

[7] Robert Burton, *The Anatomy of Melancholy*, ed. J. B. Bamborough, Thomas C. Faulkner, et al., 6 vols (Oxford: Clarendon Press, 1989–2000), i, p. lxii, 'The Argument of the Frontispeice', 4, 'I'th' under Columne there doth stand [...]'.

[8] e.g. Richard Brathwaite, *The English Gentleman* (1630); *The English Gentlewoman* (1631); and *The English Gentleman and English Gentlewoman* (1641), illus. in Johnson, *Catalogue*, Vaughan No. 6, Marshall Nos 4 and 40. Cf. James Howell, *Epistolae Hoelianae* (1645), illus. Johnson, *Catalogue*, Marshall, no. 94.

The ancient background of the practice is documented in Herford and Simpson's note.[9]

Some of the earliest of all lists of contents took the form of the so-called Canon Tables, which gave chapter numbers of parallel passages in the Gospels. Such tables are found in the paratexts of manuscript Bibles from the eighth century throughout the Middle Ages.[10] Invented by Eusebius of Caesarea (c.260–c.340), they served the purposes of both collation and memorization.[11] A common arrangement was architectural, each column of references being enclosed within the arches forming an arcade (Fig. 11). Mary Carruthers illustrates this from a late-ninth-century Gospels made in the Monastery of St Martin in Tours.[12] The memorial purpose of the arcade format has a long history, going back to ancient Roman methods of artificial memory. The *Ad Herennium* (formerly attributed to Cicero) recommended that items to be memorized should be visualized against 'backgrounds' (*loci*). In Ciceronian accounts of these *loci*, his examples regularly include the arch and the *intercolumnium* or intercolumnar space.

In the seventeenth century a great many engraved title pages featured such columns and arcades—nearly 70 per cent of those in Johnson's *Catalogue*. It seems likely that these were meant to focus the reader's memory on the contents distributed among the arches. Subsequently, merely to glance at a divided title page would serve to refresh the reader's memory.

Arcades and compartments belonged to a host of memorial devices—incipits, marginal drolleries, historiated and coloured initial capitals, marginal

[9] *Ben Jonson*, 9.315–16, citing Cicero, *Academicae quaestiones*, 2.2; *De Oratore*, 2.74; Quintilian, 11.2.

[10] See Mary Carruthers, *The Book of Memory: A Study of Memory in Medieval Culture* (Cambridge: Cambridge University Press, 1990), 248 and index, s.v. *Canon Tables*; *Columnia*; and *Intercolumnia*. See also Lina Bolzoni, *The Gallery of Memory: Literary and Iconographic Models in the Age of the Printing Press*, trans. Jeremy Parzen, Toronto Italian Studies (Toronto: University of Toronto Press, 2001), ch. 5; Alastair Fowler, 'Ut Architectura Poesis', in Clare Lapraik Guest, *Rhetoric, Theatre and the Arts of Design: Essays Presented to Roy Eriksen* (Oslo: Novus, 2008), 156–9.

[11] See Carruthers, *Book of Memory*, 139.

[12] Ibid., fig. 4. Cf. Christopher de Hamel, *A History of Illuminated Manuscripts* (1996; rev. edn, London: Phaidon, 1997), 78–9, pl. 65, from Cambridge: Corpus Christi Coll. MS 48, fo. 201ᵛ; *The Book* (2001), 17, 58, 116, 124, 125, pl. 5. A particularly magnificent example is the early ninth-century Gospels of Queen Theutberga: see Christie's Catalogue, 15 July 2015.

Fig. 11. Canon table, Cambridge CCC MS 48, fo. 201ᵛ. Courtesy of Corpus Christi College at Cambridge.

marks such as pilcrows (¶) and manicles (pointing hands)—all designed to aid memorization. Ancient authorities on artificial memory often spoke of the value of architectural columns. Columns made a title page resemble the façade of a memory palace or theatre.[13] Memory theatres such as Giulio Camillo's and Robert Fludd's facilitated memorization by providing suitable mental spaces for the purpose;[14] and a book's frontispiece was similarly meant as a locus for memorizing contents. So much is obvious from Philander Colutius's *Theatrum naturae* (1611),[15] the title page of which represent the book's themes by short texts shown as placed in a literal memory theatre.

The use of pictorial images to assist memorization was central to the art of artificial memory.[16] Only a few title pages dispensed with images, and showed the contents explicitly by lists of topics or analytic tables. These instances probably drew their inspiration from the tabular diagrams of Jean Bodin and François de Fougerolles.[17]

[13] On memory palaces, see Frances A. Yates, *The Art of Memory* (London: Routledge & Kegan Paul, 1966), ch. 6.

[14] Ibid. 336.

[15] Discussed in Ann Blair, *The Theatre of Nature: Jean Bodin and Renaissance Science* (Princeton: Princeton University Press, 1997), 173.

[16] See Carruthers, *Book of Memory*, index, s.v. *Images*; Yates, *Art of Memory*, index, s.v. *Memory: types of images*.

[17] Blair, *Theatre of Nature*, 133 (Bodin) and 162 (Fougerolles).

Later History

In the seventeenth century—'the century of the frontispiece' as the Goncourts called it—title page design was becoming simpler and broader. This can be seen in such eminent works as Francis Bacon's *Instauratio magna* (1620) and Edward Sherburne's translation of Manilius' *Astronomica* (1673) (Frontispieces 7 (p. 126), 11 (p. 156)). The content of the frontispiece might remain emblematic or mythological, but its figures and inscriptions were fewer and their import easier to grasp. Designers avoided erudite motifs, and limited symbolic attributes to those most familiar (Pan's pipes; Mercury's caduceus).

Classicizing fashions

Meanwhile, author portraits gave way to classicizing busts, particularly with ancient authors. In this, the outstanding frontispieces included those of John

Ogilby's *Aeneid* (1649) and *The Works of Virgil* (1763) translated by Christopher Pitt, Joseph Warton, and others.[1] Among modern poets, Robert Herrick had himself portrayed as a 'busto' in his 1648 frontispiece—perhaps part of his aspiration to be Anacreon's avatar. Some ancient authors still appeared as conjectural portraits; but these ran the risk of seeming implausibly realistic, like the Juvenal and Persius imagined by Barten Holyday.[2]

Generalized classical ornament now appeared everywhere, but especially in illustrative headpieces and historiated initials. The master of such ornament was Dean Aldrich of Christ Church, considered 'the only man for inventing [...] borders for a book'. His designs (still surviving) were used for Clarendon's *History of the Rebellion* (1702–4).[3] Headpieces might portray vaguely symbolic objects (as in Matthew Prior's 1718 *Poems*), again using commonplace images such as hearts and Cupids. Vignettes continued to feature, but were now unrelated to the text. The term *frontispiece* was now confusingly applied to sculptural ornaments such as the pediment over a door, or to engraved panels (*OED* 2). A famous but under-interpreted example is the pediment confronting Satan at *Paradise Lost*, 3.506: 'a kingly palace gate | with frontispiece of diamond and gold'.

Although headpieces usually had no immediate relevance to the text below them, Alexander Pope wanted his to be more than formal decorations. 'Perhaps trying to bring engraving and letterpress into a closer relationship' (as David Foxon puts it), Pope made them in effect direct illustrations, like the full-size frontispieces often facing the title page or opening of each book of a long poem. Foxon, who has closely studied Pope's design, stresses that the execution of the headpieces was personally supervised: 'It must have been

[1] For Ogilby, see *The Grolier Club's Catalogue of Original and Early Editions of Some of the Poetical and Prose Works of English Writers from Langland to Prior*, 4 vols in 1 (Holland Press, 1964), no. 640; for Pitt, see *OHLTE* iii. 167; Stuart Gillespie, *English Translation and Classical Reception* (Oxford: Wiley-Blackwell, 2011), index, s.v. *Christopher Pitt*.

[2] See John Dryden, *The Poems: Vol. 4: 1693–1696*, ed. Paul Hammond and David Hopkins (Harlow: Pearson, 2000), pl. 2, from *Decimus Junius Juvenalis and Aulus Persius Flaccus, Translated and Illustrated, as well with Sculpture* [engravings] *as Notes, by Barten Holyday* (Oxford, 1673).

[3] David Foxon, *Pope and the Early Eighteenth-Century Book Trade*, rev. James McLaverty (Oxford: Clarendon Press, 1991), 81 and fig. 33.

Pope, for example, who laid on their designer the difficult task of producing a long narrow headpiece in place of the traditional upright plate' (p. 71). Pope was certainly familiar with the current fashion for headpieces and initials: in a letter of 16 August 1714 he writes to Charles Jervas: 'Homer advances so fast, that he begins to look about for the ornaments he is to appear in, like a modish modern author.'[4] Pope's preference for direct illustration seems to have been a settled conviction—doubtless based on his early enthusiasm for Ogilby's 1660 Homer. Joseph Spence tells how Ogilby's translation was

one of the first large poems that ever Mr Pope read, and he still spoke of the pleasure it then gave him, with a sort of rapture only on reflecting on it. 'It was that great edition with pictures. I was then about eight years old. This led me to Sandys's Ovid, which I liked extremely.'[5]

More recent models included Jacob Tonson the elder's *Caesar* (1712).[6]

The illustrative headpieces were not altogether successful: they looked too deep for the quarto format Pope had selected for his Homer and Shakespeare. Nevertheless this format became through Pope's influence almost obligatory for luxury books.[7] The same disproportion between headpiece and text appears in Joseph Trapp's *Aeneid* (1718–20) and Milton's *Works* (1720), originally intended for a folio format.[8] A happier proportion, deeper than Pope's, appears in the headpiece by Louis Chéron for Rowe's folio Lucan (1718). But Pope's example largely determined the taste for illustrative headpieces.

Illustrations

Illustrated editions of the classics eventually displaced the emblematic frontispiece. This development began early, in Italy, with the many illustrated

[4] Alexander Pope, *The Correspondence*, ed. George Sherburn, 5 vols (Oxford, 1956), i. 243.
[5] Joseph Spence, *Observations, Anecdotes and Characters of Books and Men*, ed. James M. Osborn, 2 vols (Oxford: Clarendon Press, 1966), no. 30; cf. Foxon, *Book Trade*, 78.
[6] Ibid. 74, fig. 34.
[7] Ibid. 63–4, 71.
[8] Ibid. 76, figs 37, 38; 74, fig. 36; 71.

Dantes and with Girolamo Porro's *Orlando Furioso* (1584). Sandys's 1632 *Metamorphosis*, although published in America, had a seminal influence in England. So had John Ogilby's edition of Virgil's *Georgics* when it was reprinted in 1654 with forty-four fine etchings by Hollar after Francis Clein's designs—perhaps the most ambitious illustrated volume yet published in England. By the eighteenth century Chaucer and Shakespeare and other vernacular classics underwent similar refashioning.

Illustrated editions of the *Canterbury Tales* gave occasions to reinterpret the Gothic Chaucer. Typical are *The Works of Jeoffrey Chaucer*, edited by John Urry (1721), and the Chaucer in John Bell's *Poets of Great Britain* series (1782). The neo-Gothic engravings in these created romantic ideas of the medieval Chaucer in a way very different from the translations and imitations of Dryden, Pope, and others.[9] The frontispieces by Thomas Stothard (1755–1834) retained few residues of emblem or symbol: he discreetly modernized costumes, retaining only an occasional anachronistic ruff. Similarly with Shakespeare. Here the influential artist was the entrepreneur and engraver John Boydell (1720–1804), who published a series of prints illustrating Shakespeare. His over-ambitious project of commissioning paintings on Shakespearean subjects from the foremost history painters proved financially disastrous. But his *Shakespeare Gallery* illustrations valuably demonstrated various technical methods. In particular, Boydell popularized mezzotint, making way in the following century for the masterpieces of John Martin.

Boydell's illustrations aimed at—and helped to create—a popular market. More popular still were the chapbook editions of popular ballads, typically illustrated on the title page itself with very rough woodcuts. Humble as it was, this form of publication (circulated by itinerant dealers) held great attractions for Wordsworth and Coleridge. Coleridge wrote to his wife that he would many times rather have 'Christabel' 'printed at Soulby's on the true Ballad Paper' than in a luxury edition.[10] Soulby printed several popular chapbooks on coarse paper—for example, *The Wandering Jew* and *Tom Hickathrift*

[9] See Alice Miskimin, 'The Illustrated Eighteenth-Century Chaucer', *Modern Philology*, 77 (1979), 26–55.

[10] Paul Cheshire, '"I lay too many Eggs": Coleridge's "Ostrich Carelessness" and the Problem of Publication', *Coleridge Bulletin*, NS 23 (2004), 11, figs 5, 6.

(*c.*1800). Somewhere between this lowly form and the exquisite vignettes of Thomas Bewick (1753–1828) came such modest general illustrations as those in M. Le Grand's *Fabliaux* (1796), printed by W. Bulmer and Co.'s Shakespeare press.[11] Wordsworth and Coleridge enthused over the illustrations in Le Grand, which offered a model for Coleridge's 'Christabel'. Wordsworth wrote 'I long to have the book in my hand it will be such a Beauty'; and Coleridge made special mention of the attraction the vignettes had for him: 'little Drawings engraved or cut in wood [...] head- and tail-pieces.'[12] The edition got the length of a proposal to Longman, but fell through when Coleridge's rapid progress turned out to be imaginary.

Vignettes might appear on the title page, as in Le Grand's 1796 *Fabliaux*. It was, after all, 'the century of the vignette'.[13] But the standard eighteenth-century title-page design was typographical, often without any ornament whatso ever. Any illustration was moved to a frontispiece facing the title page.

Meanwhile, *front* and *frontispiece* went through a range of new meanings. At first architectural terms for the principal or decorated façade of a building, they came to be applied metaphorically to a book's '*front* matter' or paratext, including the title page itself and any illustrations it might have. Later, *frontispiece* more specifically referred to a sculptural panel or pediment, as in Pope's 'ornaments'—frontispieces in *OED*'s sense 2. In 1721, Nathan Bailey's *Universal Etymological English Dictionary* comprehended all these: 'frontispiece: the Title or first Page of a Book done in picture'.[14] The modern sense of *frontispiece* had now emerged: an illustration facing the title page (*OED* 4). *OED*'s 1682 example, from John Lithgow's *Travels* ('the Frontis-piece is my Effigies'), refers to an author portrait facing the title page.

The nineteenth-century book brought a strong counter-movement in book design. Instead of austerely simple title pages of plain typography, there came a return to decorative, illustrated, even narrative paratexts.

---

[11] Cheshire, '"Eggs"', fig. 1; M. le Grand, *Fabliaux or Tales, Abridged from French Manuscripts of the XIITH and XIIITH Centuries* (London: Bulmer, 1796).

[12] Cheshire, '"Eggs"', 7–8, figs 1–3.

[13] *OCB* 140.

[14] Bailey's dictionary had 40,000 entries, and in a later edition was used as a base text by Samuel Johnson. See A. P. Cowie, *The Oxford History of English Lexicography*, 2 vols (Oxford: Clarendon Press, 2009), i. 80–1, 150–2.

Narrative illustration

The cause of this large change may be put down to the growth of narrative publication. The late eighteenth century saw relatively little narrative, although a few outstanding novels have given a different impression. Defoe's output was over by the 1720s: in the 1730s and 1740s there were only Richardson and Fielding: and in the 1750s and 1760s only Smollett and Sterne. The next forty years, apart from Gothic romances, knew just two novelists, Fanny Burney and Maria Edgeworth. Only after Jane Austen (1811–18) and Walter Scott (1814–32) did the stream of narrative fiction became a torrent.

Eighteenth-century illustrations were often generalized or decorative, whereas those in Victorian novels tended to be 'direct' (to adopt Ruth Luborsky's terminology).[15] In the earlier century, direct narrative illustration was mostly limited, as we have seen, to illustrated editions of Chaucer, Shakespeare, and the ancient classics.[16] But now widespread illustration began of vernacular literature and even of contemporary fiction. This change was furthered by the practice of issuing novels—and even non-fiction—in illustrated monthly parts. A notable example is Pierce Egan's *Life in London* (1800), illustrated by Cruikshank. Dickens's *Posthumous Papers of the Pickwick Club*, issued after many vicissitudes in 1836–7, with illustrations by Hablôt Knight Browne (1815–82) under the pseudonym 'Phiz'. Serial publication soon established his popularity.

Both the monthly parts and the volume edition of *Pickwick* had illustrated title pages.[17] The title page of the volume edition shows Sam Weller in the doorway of the Marquis of Granby, an inn belonging to Weller senior. Sam watches his father immersing Mr Stiggins (a dissenting preacher) in a horse trough—an incident from chapter 51. This is a direct illustration of the moment when 'he at length permitted Mr Stiggins to withdraw his head from the trough' but before he throws his energy 'into one most complicated

---

[15] Ruth Samson Luborsky, 'Connections and Disconnections between Images and Texts: The Case of Secular Tudor Book Illustration', *Word and Image*, 3 (1987), 74.

[16] See Stuart Sillars, *The Illustrated Shakespeare 1709–1875* (Cambridge: Cambridge University Press, 2008).

[17] Cave and Ayad, 190–1.

Fig. 12. Mr Stiggins immersed, Dickens, *Pickwick Papers* (1837). Dunstan B 712a, Title Page. Courtesy of the Bodleian Libraries, The University of Oxford.

kick' (Fig. 12). No picture can represent more than a moment in time, so that in a sense no picture can tell a story. But the illustration of a well-chosen moment can suggest what is about to happen, prompting viewers to supply the continuation (in this case a kick). A single picture can thus encapsulate a whole anecdote.[18]

The frontispiece of the volume edition also shows Sam Weller, this time sitting at ease with Mr Pickwick. As always he wears his 'grey coat [...] a black hat with a cockade to it, a pink striped waistcoat, light breeches and gaiters'. This illustration seems less directly representative of a single moment in the story. It could be called allusive: as in many political cartoons the figures are recognizable and the situation typical, but the narrative references are broad.

Illustration and narrative extended even to the covers of books in the elaborate decoration of publishers' bindings.[19] These were pioneered in children's books such as the 1882 *Robinson Crusoe*.[20] They are so characteristic of their period as to be used sometimes to lend Victorian atmosphere to a modern book, as with Julian Barnes's *Arthur and George* (2005). Illustrated dust covers have extended this possibility farther. The innovator in this direction was Sir William Stirling-Maxwell, who introduced illustrated wrappers for monumental volumes such as his *Antwerp Delivered* (1878).[21]

Retrospective Gothic

Modern literature with so many illustrations had not been seen since the Middle Ages and the seventeenth century.[22] It is commonplace that a large proportion of nineteenth-century art was retrospective—inspired by the life

---

[18] John Harthan, *The History of the Illustrated Book: The Western Tradition* (London: Thames and Hudson, 1981), 201; cf. Luborsky, 'Connections and Disconnections' (1987), 74.

[19] See Edmund M. B. King, *Victorian Decorated Trade Bindings 1830–1880* (London: British Library, 2003).

[20] See Cave and Ayad, 178–9, 194–5.

[21] e.g. Sir William Stirling-Maxwell, *Antwerp Delivered* [...] *Illustrated with Facsimiles of Designs by Martin de Vos* [...] (Edinburgh: David Douglas, 1878); *The Chief Victories of* [...] *Charles the Fifth, Designed by M. Heemskerck* (London and Edinburgh: privately printed for the editor, 1870).

[22] See Claire M. L. Bourne, '"High Designe": Beaumont and Fletcher Illustrated', *English Literary Renaissance*, 44 (2014), 275–327.

and literature of the Middle Ages.[23] In visual art this certainly rings true of the narrative painting of the Pre-Raphaelites. In poetry, one thinks of Coleridge's 'Christabel', Keats's 'The Eve of St Agnes', and Tennyson's *Idylls of the King* and 'The Lady of Shallott'; in prose, the many historical romances, from Charles Reade's *The Cloister and the Hearth* to George Eliot's *Romola*, speak for themselves. Conan Doyle rated *The White Company* and *The Fortunes of Nigel* above the Sherlock Holmes stories. And in architecture, incontestably, count the huge number of Gothic buildings.[24]

In the nineteenth century, even the pages of books were made to look medieval. William Blake, for example, in his highly original 'illuminated printing' or relief etchings, returned to the art of medieval manuscripts: his designs evoked the interlinear decoration of a medieval page. In popular printing, too, the same fashion prevailed. Henry Noel Humphreys' *Miracles of Our Lord* (1848) reprised the familiar elements of medieval books: floral initial capitals and interlaced borders.[25] And W. Kent and Co. published a gift book, *Three Gems in One Setting* (1860), containing poems by Tennyson illustrated by Anne Lydia Bond. Its pages had floral borders, clearly designed to suggest manuscript formats.[26]

The fashion culminated in William Morris's Kelmscott Chaucer, illustrated—or illuminated—by the Pre-Raphaelite artist Edward Burne-Jones. Morris used Gothic fonts, decorated initial capitals, and elaborate, retrospective borders. Theodore Low de Vinne, the American authority on the title page, greatly admired Morris's designs although not always his influence. He regarded Morris as 'a medievalist thoroughly saturated with the spirit of the fifteenth century', but thought it 'a great misfortune that the Morris style has been so often imitated, for it was devised by Morris for medieval books or

---

[23] See Alice Chandler, *A Dream of Order: The Medieval Ideal in Nineteenth-Century English* (Lincoln, NE: University of Nebraska Press, 1971); Michael Alexander, *The Middle Ages in Modern England* (New Haven, CT: Yale University Press, 2007).

[24] See Simon Thurley, *The Building of England* (London: Collins, 2013), 416–19; index, s.v. *gothic; gothic revival*.

[25] Gordon N. Ray, *The Illustrator and the Book in England from 1791 to 1914* (Oxford: Pierpont Morgan Library and Oxford University Press, 1976), 146–7; Harthan, *Illustrated Book* (1981), pl. xix.

[26] Mathieu Lommen, *The Book of Books: 500 Years of Graphic Innovation* (London: Thames & Hudson, 2012), 258–9.

subjects, and should be used for them exclusively'.[27] De Vinne's view is too extreme. At the very least, 'medieval' needs to be enlarged to include 'medievalizing'. What could be more appropriate, for example, than Morris's design for Dante Gabriel Rossetti's *Hand and Soul* (1895)?[28]

Morris's Kelmscott Press was among the best of the private presses that were to produce many of the finest books of the twentieth century. (Others include the Doves, Gregynog, Golden Cockerel, and Nonesuch Presses.) Private presses could afford to be experimental and unconventional, although their letterpress equipment tended to have been discarded by commercial publishers. This was not inappropriate, for their designs were at best imbued with a profound sense of book history.[29]

Conclusions

As one surveys the chameleon history of the title page, two conflicting patterns stand out. First, certain features have persisted over long periods of time, although they have by no means been regular in any. An example is the author portrait, which can be found in ancient manuscripts, in printed frontispieces, and in the wrappers of many contemporary books. Other constants are the title (or at least the incipit) and the author's name. Since printing began, information about the publisher has been a dependable feature; although its position has varied, from the colophon to the title leaf—first the title page, more recently the verso of the title page.

A second pattern is one of widely ranging variation: from the crowded first page of some manuscript books to the bareness of the eighteenth-century and modern typographical title page. So predictable has the contemporary title page become that readers understandably tend to pass over it.

---

[27] Theodore Low de Vinne, *A Treatise on Title-Pages* [...] (New York: Century Co., 1902), 390, 398.

[28] See Lommen, *Book of Books*, 276–7.

[29] See *OCB* ii. 1055–7.

Frontispieces & Commentaries

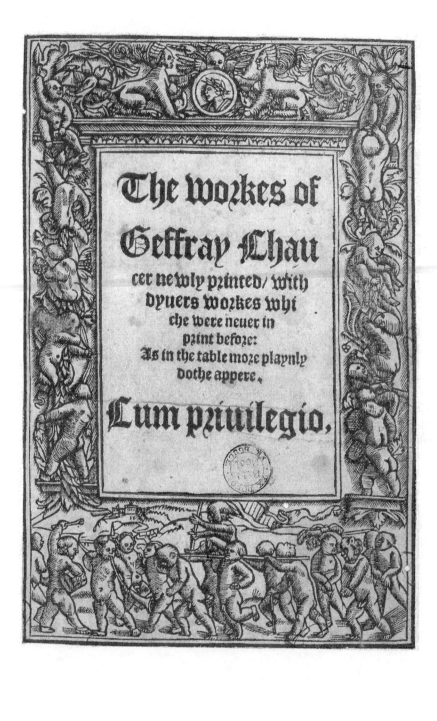

The workes of Geffray Chau
cer newly printed/ with
dyuers workes whi
che were neuer in
print before:
As in the table more playnly
dothe appere,

Cum priuilegio,

Geffray Chaucer
THE WORKES
1532

Considering the number of works it includes, William Thynne's has a good claim to be the first edition of Chaucer's complete works. In the same year as Thynne's Chaucer, Thomas Berthelet's edition of Gower had a title-page frame that has rightly been described as modern.[1] But the more ambitious title page of Thynne's Chaucer gives a more complex impression. The title—*The workes of Geffray Chaucer newly printed, with divers workes whiche were never in print before: As in the table more plainly dothe appere. Cum privilegio*—is inscribed in Gothic black letter in an architectural frame with a moulded cornice.

Appropriately for an author who inaugurated a new age of literature, the title page has both medieval and Renaissance features. Its title border derived

---

[1] Lotte Hellinga, *William Caxton and Early Printing in England* (London: British Library, 2010), 186, fig. 109a.

from a well-established, broad type of illuminated liturgical and calendrical manuscripts; whereas this particular border had classical and Renaissance models.[2] There are many signs of wear and recutting; but the high quality of Holbein's original woodcut shows through. The English title page reuses the fine title border of the *Epigrammata* of Erasmus, published by Johann Froben of Basle in 1518.[3] Holbein's border belonged to the brief period when the Frobens' Basle press was an important centre of printing and illustration. Both Erasmus and Holbein worked for Johann Froben (*c.*1460–1527).

In the sides of the border a dozen putti climb over the swags and foliage. In the lower border a triumphal procession of fifteen putti moves from R to L: a vanguard of four, including a drummer and horn player; six others carrying a seventh who holds aloft a banner; and, bringing up the rear, four putti bound as captives. The top border is dominated by two sphinx-like grotesques flanked by interlaced foliage, while at the centre a winged cherub supports a circular frame.

This title frame is used not only for the main title page but also for several subsequent part titles: for *The Canterbury Tales*; for *The Romaunt of the Rose*; for *Troylus and Creseyde*; for *Boetius de Consolatione Philosophie*; and other individual works, not least Usk's *The Testament of Love*, which is known only from this edition.

Portraits

There was no obvious printed portrait of Chaucer until Thomas Speght's 1598 edition. But the cherub above the cornice in Thynne's title page holds a roundel framing the laureate head of a generic author, which serves as a portrait of Chaucer. The volume also has cuts illustrating the Canterbury

---

[2] *The Grolier Club's Catalogue of Original and Early Editions of Some of the Poetical and Prose Works of English Writers from Langland to Prior*, 4 vols in 1 (London: Holland Press, 1964), no. 39; see Introduction: Historical Settings and Borders.

[3] Stanley Morison and Kenneth Day, *The Typographic Book 1450–1935* (London: Ernest Benn, 1963), 38, pl. 44; Alfred Forbes Johnson, *German Renaissance Title-Borders* (Oxford: Bibliographical Society and Oxford University Press, 1929); R. B. McKerrow and P. S. Ferguson, *Title-Page Borders Used in England and Scotland 1485 to 1640* (Oxford: Bibliographical Society and Oxford University Press, 1932).

pilgrims (mostly second states of the cuts in Caxton's 1483 edition, STC 5083): knight and squire; miller (repeated as ploughman); reeve; cook; man of law; merchant (repeated as summoner); manciple; wife of Bath; friar; clerk (repeated as canon's yeoman); Franklin (repeated as pardoner); second nun (repeated as prioress); doctor; shipman; parson.[4] In a sense these cuts can be seen as author portraits, since they portray the fictional authors or tellers of their tales.

Editor and publisher

William Thynne, alias Boteville (d. 1546), was a successful courtier in the household of Henry VIII. From obscure origins, Thynne emerges in 1524 as second clerk of the royal kitchen, an important office usually assigned to a literate person if not a gentleman. In two years he had risen to be chief clerk, with an annuity of £10, and by 1528 he was bailiff and keeper of Beaudley Park. By 1529 he was collector of customs on wool and fleeces in London, and receiver-general of the earldom of March. He rose to be Henry's clerk controller, and eventually a master of the king's household and officer of the counting house. Francis Thynne gives much information about his father's life—including the duties of a kitchen clerk—in his *Animadversions* on Speght's edition of Chaucer.[5]

In his second career as a man of letters, William Thynne was the first editor (in something like the modern sense) of Chaucer's complete works. His single volume collection (STC 5068) shows him practising what would now be called textual criticism. He used as many as twenty-five Chaucer manuscripts, some of which survive at the second Longleat house, marked up for the printer. They include the important Longleat MS 258 and the Glasgow University MS Hunterian V. 3. 7.

---

[4] See Luborsky and Ingram, i. 276–7; Edward Hodnett, *English Woodcuts 1480–1535* (rev. edn, Oxford: Oxford University Press, 1975); D. Carlson, 'Woodcut Illustrations of *The Canterbury Tales*, 1483–1602', *The Library*, 6th ser., 19 (1957), 25–67, esp. 63.

[5] Francis Thynne, *Animadversions upon the Annotacions* [...] *of Chaucers Workes* [...] *Reprinted in* [...] *1598*, EETS, OS 9 (1875; London: Oxford University Press, 1965). See also A. S. G. Edwards, in *ODNB*.

William Thynne based his Chaucer collection on earlier printed editions by William Caxton, Richard Pynson, and Wynkyn de Worde. Like them, he included several non-Chaucerian works—by Robert Henryson (*Testament of Cresseid*), Thomas Hoccleve, Sir Richard Roos, and John Lydgate. Thynne was prevented by Wolsey from including the Protestant polemic *The Plowman's Tale*, but it was added to his edition in later reprints. Altogether there were six different editions of Thynne's Chaucer, from 1542 to 1550 (?). He published the first editions of *The Book of the Duchess*, *The Legend of Good Women*, *Boece*, and *The Treatise on the Astrolabe*. Thynne's Chaucer was the basis of John Stowe's (1561), as Stowe's in turn was the basis of Speght's (1598). Like other great publishers, Thynne was a patron of literature. John Skelton is said to have written most of 'Colin Clout' at Thynne's house.

Printer

The printer was Thomas Godfray, who worked in London, at Temple Bar and in the Old Bailey, from 1531(?) to 1536. His 1532 Chaucer edition is one of only two imprints to which he gave a date. Godfray's output includes translations from reformers (Valla, Erasmus, and Martin Bucer); selections from the Bible; *The History of King Boccus* (1537); and a poem on the Battle of Agincourt. Some of his type, for example a 94mm textura ('church type' or formal Gothic letter) came from Pynson; some (woodcut initials in *Boccus*, the 'L' in his Chaucer, and a 91mm textura) belonged to Robert Saltwood the Canterbury monk and patron.[6] Perhaps Godfray deliberately intended an archaizing effect.

How did Godfray come by the Holbein title border? Since Godfray obtained his textura type from Pynson, and Pynson is known to have had business relations with Froben of Basle,[7] it seems likely that Froben's text border came to Godfray via Pynson.

---

[6] See *STC* 3. 69; Frank Isaac, *English Printers' Types of the Sixteenth Century* (Oxford: Oxford University Press, 1936), pl. 30; Hellinga, *William Caxton and Early Printing*, 185–8.

[7] Isaac, *Printers' Types*, 4, 15.

The Byble in Englyshe, that is to saye the content of all the holy scrypture, bothe of ý olde and newe testament, truly translated after the veryte of the hebrue and Greke textes, by ý dylygent studye of dyuerse excellent learned men, expert in the forsayde tonges.

Prynted by Rychard Grafton & Edward Whitchurch.

Cum priuilegio ad imprimendum solum.
1539.

THE GREAT BIBLE

1539

O f the bibles used in Tudor England, the most important were the Latin
Vulgate ('popular'), translated by St Jerome (d. 420) and dominant
throughout the Middle Ages; reforming translations by William Tyndale
(1525, 1530) and by Miles Coverdale (1535, 1537); the Great Bible (1539, 1540,
'Cranmer's'); the Geneva translation (1560) with reforming marginal comments; the Bishops' Bible (1568, Archbishop Matthew Parker's revision of
the Great Bible); and the Roman Catholic Douai–Rheims New Testament
(1582) and Old Testament (1610). The Coverdale–Tyndale translation was
published as by Thomas Matthew.[1] After the death of Henry VIII, restric-

---

[1] On these versions and their relations to the King James Bible, see Jaroslav Pelikan, *The
Reformation of the Bible: The Bible of the Reformation* (New Haven: Yale University Press,
1996); Christopher de Hamel, *The Book: A History of the Bible* (New York and London:
Phaidon, 2001), and *Bibles: An Illustrated History from Papyrus to Print* (Oxford: Bodleian

tions on the printing and importing of bibles were removed. Under Queen Mary (1553–8), however, no bibles at all were printed—not even Roman Catholic ones—although licensing of the Great Bible was not repealed. Under Queen Elizabeth, any bible could be printed and owned.

The various sixteenth-century English translations differed little in substance. Differences were mostly local, in effect different choices between near synonyms: *church/congregation*; *priest/elder*; *chalice/cup*; *charity/love*. Reforming versions determinedly went back before the Vulgate to the earliest witnesses (Greek and Hebrew), aiming at the most accurate translation recent scholarship could devise. Marginal comments, however, and tendentious italics within the text often made a point of ideological differences. Consequently, when Henry VIII (on 5 September 1538) commanded that a copy of the bible in English should be placed in every church in England, he wanted a version without inflammatory marginalia. Coverdale's translation from Latin and Luther's German (printed perhaps in Cologne and imported) was selling well; but the king commanded a further, uncontroversial revision of Coverdale for public use in churches. This was the Great Bible (so called from its large size, 237 × 235 mm): a lectern bible for public reading. Like other sixteenth-century versions, it was a composite translation by committee, instructed by the king's deputy, Thomas Cromwell, and overseen by Coverdale (1488–1568) and Archbishop Cranmer (1489–1556).

Printing

The Great Bible was initially to be printed in Paris. This was not because there were no good English printers, but because no English printers had the equipment or the paper to print in the large size called for. François Regnault was doubtless chosen as a dependable exporter with a record of cooperation with English printers. Two English printers, Edward Whitchurch and Richard

Library, 2011); David Daniell, *The Bible in English* (New Haven and London: Yale University Press, 2003); Helen Moore and Julian Reid (eds), *Manifold Greatness: The Making of the King James Bible* (Oxford: Bodleian Library, 2011); David Crystal, *Begat: The King James Bible and the English Language* (Oxford: Oxford University Press, 2010); Gordon Campbell, *Bible: The Story of the King James Version 1611–2011* (Oxford: Oxford University Press, 2010).

Grafton, were sent to Paris to supervise the printing, 'in as privy manner as might be'.[2] In return for producing acceptable bibles largely financed by themselves, they received a generic privilege—in effect a monopoly.

At first all went well, and samples were sent home. But in October 1538 the authorities got wind of the project, and Regnault was twice summoned by the Inquisition, who confiscated 2,000 sheets. Meanwhile in England there was opposition to the Great Bible's containing any annotation whatsoever. Cromwell, deeply committed to 'his' bible, invested £400 of his own money in the project, and personally negotiated for the release of the sheets. In this he had the help of the Constable of France, and of Edmund Bonner, bishop of London and a supporter of bible translation.[3] But a series of engagements between German, French, and English ships, with subsequent legal actions, led to strained relations with France and threatened the Great Bible project.[4] Fortunately the French were shown to have been in the wrong, and in the end a compromise was reached.

Presses, paper, and type were bought from Regnault and transported to London, where most of the printing was done. Regnault's printed contribution was only 159 edition sheets, including parts 1 and 2 (Genesis to Job). The Great Bible was to be sold unbound for 10 shillings, a very low price. But Whitchurch and Grafton hoped to recoup their investment from what amounted to a monopoly of printing future bibles.

Printers

In the 1530s, Edward Whitchurch (d. 1562) was a member of the Haberdashers' Company. Later a printer and bookseller, he and Richard Grafton acted as publishers of the Matthew Bible translated by John Rogers and printed in Antwerp by Matthias Crom. Whitchurch again joined with Grafton in supervising printing of the Great Bible in Paris. When the project was relocated to London, they themselves acted as printers, assisted by Thomas Berthelet, the King's Printer. From 1539 to 1541, Whitchurch and Grafton

---

[2] Peter W. M. Blayney, *The Stationers' Company and the Printers of London, 1501–1557*, 2 vols (Cambridge: Cambridge University Press, 2013), i. 361, 364.

[3] Ibid. i. 363, 365, 367.   [4] See Daniell, *The Bible in English*, 201–2.

published six editions of the Great Bible together with New Testaments and primers. Under Edward VI their privilege to print service books was renewed, and they published the early editions of the 1549 Book of Common Prayer.

Whitchurch consistently worked for evangelical reform. He and Grafton were more than once arrested, and sometimes imprisoned, for not attending confession or for printing heretical books. But Whitchurch also published less controversial works such as Roger Ascham's *Toxophilus* (1545), Katherine Parr's *Lamentacion of a Sinner* (1547), Erasmus's *Paraphrases* (1548), Sternhold and Hopkins's metrical psalter, and the first book printed in Welsh.

Married at least once, Whitchurch had a son and three daughters. The location of his earliest workplace is uncertain, perhaps at the Sign of the Bible in St Paul's Churchyard in 1540. About 1544 he was at the south side of St Mary Aldermanbury Church and at Old Jewry, and in 1545 he moved to the Sun in Fleet Street, which had once belonged to Wynkyn de Worde. After the accession of Mary, he probably fled to Germany. After Cranmer's execution in 1555, Whitchurch married his widow. He retired in 1562 to a house in Camberwell.

Richard Grafton (*c.*1511–73), a Shrewsbury man, was apprenticed to John Blage, grocer to Thomas Cranmer and a man of evangelical sympathies. Grafton became free of the Grocers' Company in 1534: he was a merchant adventurer with Antwerp connections. With Thomas Cromwell as patron, Grafton put his commercial expertise and capital at the disposal of the reformers. Like Whitchurch, he was involved in producing the Coverdale–Tyndale translation printed pseudonymously as by Thomas Matthew. Grafton acted as commercial agent to the Great Bible project, with Coverdale as editor. After Cromwell had been executed in 1540, Grafton was three times imprisoned for publishing material critical of the new regime, but released by order of the king. On Henry VIII's death, Grafton became printer to King Edward VI. With Whitchurch, he published the *Book of Common Prayer* (1549) and John Marbecke's *Concordance* to the Bible (1550).

When Edward VI died in 1553, Grafton sided with Lady Jane Grey's faction, and under Mary he lost his position of royal printer. But he was commissioned to arrange pageants for Philip and Mary's royal entry into London (1554). He also produced pageants for Queen Elizabeth's coronation in 1558. Grafton was twice Warden of the Grocers' Company, and sat in Parliament as a London MP (1557) and MP for Coventry (1563). Even after he had given up printing, he continued to live in Greyfriars.

Grafton's son-in-law Richard Tottel (d. 1594) inherited his types and woodcuts, and it was Tottel who issued Grafton's *Abridgement of the Chronicles of England* (1562–3). Grafton himself compiled and published *Manuell of Chronicles* (1565) and several other works of a similar character. He attempted to secure a monopoly of such abridgements, in fierce rivalry with Thomas Marsh and John Stow. The battle was exacerbated by Grafton's financial difficulties: despite his many connections with the City of London and his lenient treatment by the courts, he was still in debt in 1569.

François Regnault (*c.*1496–1540?) was a key figure in the import trade.[5] Of more than a hundred books printed overseas for the English market, he printed at least a quarter.[6] In 1534, even Thomas Berthelet's new Latin translation of Psalms and Ecclesiastes was commissioned from Regnault's press. So Regnault was the natural choice as printer of the Great Bible, and later as a source of equipment.

Tableau

At the top, God is shown blessing the publication of the Great Bible and the bible-reading community it is intended for. He is not exactly crouching,[7] but certainly seems a distant figure by comparison with Henry VIII and his officials. Henry distributes copies of the bible (*verbum Dei*) to Archbishop Cranmer and Bishop Bonner (L), who have laid aside their mitres in the king's presence, and to Thomas Cromwell (R), who is also bare-headed. Christopher de Hamel compares St Jerome's distribution of the Latin bible to monks in the Vivian Bible of Charles the Bold.[8]

In the middle register (L), Cranmer, now mitred, hands a bible to a bareheaded cleric. Cranmer can be identified from his coat of arms, framed by a

---

[5] See Hugh William Davies, *Devices of the Early Printers 1457–1560* (London: Grafton, 1935), 330, 646; *STC* 3. 144.

[6] Blayney, *The Stationers' Company*, i. 319.

[7] As described by Daniell, *The Bible in English*, 206.

[8] De Hamel, *The Book: A History of the Bible*, 38, pl. 21.

laurel wreath. On the other side of the title inset, Cromwell does likewise (R). After his fall and execution, his arms, framed by the Garter, were replaced by a blank in subsequent editions. The vertical sequence gives a clear impression of hierarchy: God to Henry, Henry to Cranmer, Cranmer to priest.

In the lowest register, a cleric (L) is shown preaching—according to Daniell, *extempore*. But, although no bible is visible, a scroll indicates he is remembering 1 Timothy 2: 1–2. His congregation, although not of professional people, is far from being 'rabble', as Daniell has called it. It is a carefully varied crowd. As their costume shows, they are men and women of all conditions: mothers and children, young and old, laity and clergy. One is a soldier, and some are prisoners. Many have speech-scrolls, cheering *vivat rex* ('God save the king'); but some cheer in English. One *vivat rex* scroll clearly refers to those in prison. All are glad to witness the distribution of the Great Bible—all, except for an angry devil at the foot of the page, slinking away in disgust.

Inscriptions

Much has been made of the use of Latin in the title page of an English bible. It was probably calculated to calm the more conservative bishops. Bishop Gardiner of Winchester thought the only acceptable bible was the Vulgate. Besides, as the preamble shows, Henry was concerned in case the 'lower sort' would cause dissention by quarrelling over erroneous opinions. The terrible Anabaptist rising at Münster in 1534 was in everyone's mind.

In the upper registers allusions to many biblical texts, all in Latin, are inscribed on scrolls. Most of these refer to the Vulgate text; but others vary from it, either by error or because they refer to some other version or for the purpose of the allusion. From God, a veritable labyrinth of floral banderoles issue, containing two texts: Isaiah 55: 11, *verbum meum quod egredietur de ore meo, non revertet ad me vacuum, sed faciet quaecumque volui* ('my word [...] that goeth forth out of my mouth: it shall not return unto me void, but it shall accomplish that which I please'); Acts 13: 22, *inveni virum iuxta cor meum qui facit omnes voluntates meas* ('I have found a man after mine own heart, which shall fulfil all my will'). Immediately below, issuing from Henry VIII, are three ordinary scrolls bearing the texts 1 Timothy 4: 11, *haec praecipe et doce* ('These things command and teach'); Daniel 6: 26, *A me constitutum est decretum ut in universo imperio et regno meo, tremiscant et paveant Deum Danielis: ipse est enim Deum viventem* ('I make a decree, That in every dominion of my kingdom men tremble and fear before the God of Daniel: for he is the living God'); and Deuteronomy 1: 16–17, *quod iustum est iudicate* ('judge righteously [...] hear the small as well as the great'). The scroll immediately above Cromwell's head is from Vulgate Psalm 118, *verbum tuum.*

In the middle register, on either side of the framed title inscription, are two further speech ribbons. Cranmer (L), handing the bible to a priest, commands, on the authority of 1 Peter 5: 2, *pascite qui in vobis est gregem Dei* ('Feed the flock of God which is among you'). A scroll above Cromwell's head (R) is from Vulgate Psalm 33: 15, *Diverte a malo, et fac bonum; inquire pacem, et persequere eam* (Psalm 34: 14, 'Depart from evil, and do good: seek peace, and pursue it').

In the lower register, a preacher's scroll quotes 1 Timothy 2: 1–2, *obsecro igitur primum omnium fieri obsecrationes, orationes, postulationes, gratiarum actiones, pro omnibus hominibus; pro regibus* etc. ('I exhort, therefore, that, first of all, supplications, prayers, intercessions, and giving of thanks, be made for all men; for kings').

Designer

The design of the Great Bible title page has been attributed to a French illuminator, the Master of François de Rohan;[9] also to Holbein, or at least to the School of Holbein (for Holbein's own distinctive style is absent). But the political content dominates aesthetic considerations. Any reforming Protestant such as Whitchurch would have been capable of assembling the biblical inscriptions. It is likely, however, that ultimate responsibility for the title page lay with Cromwell himself.

---

[9] De Hamel, *Bibles: An Illustrated History,* item 53.

ΠΛΗΡΑ · ΠΛΗΡΑ · ΠΛΗΡΑ

GENERAL AND RARE MEMORIALS

pertayning to the Perfect Arte of

NAVIGATION:

Annexed to the PARADOXAL *Cumpas, in Playne :
now first published : 24. yeres, after the first
Inuention thereof.*

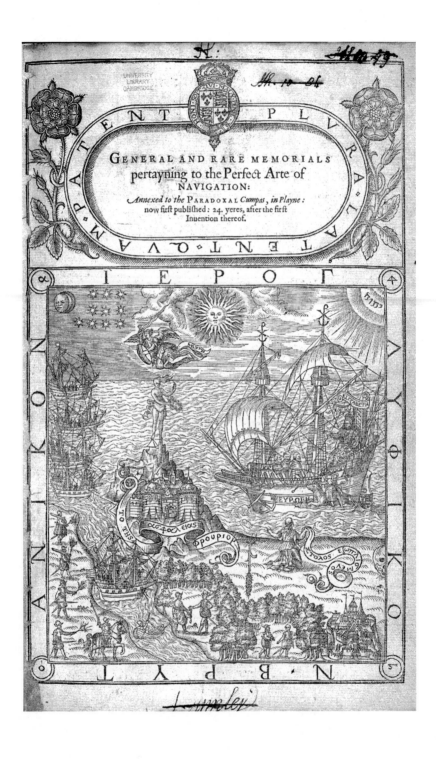

ΙΕΡΟΓΛΥΦΙΚΟΝ · ΒΡΥΤΑΝΙΚΟΝ

John Dee
GENERAL AND RARE
MEMORIALS
1577

Many think of John Dee (1527–1609) as an eccentric figure: astrologer, alchemist, conjurer, and necromancer. But he was much more mainstream than this may suggest. Magic might then be early science; Dee was an enthusiastic Copernican as early as 1556, and Renaissance alchemy led to modern chemistry. Dee's polymath erudition is beyond dispute. He was a complete Renaissance man: mathematician, geographer, astronomer, antiquarian, scholar, and magician.[1] Benefiting from the dispersal of the monastic libraries, he collected one of the largest private libraries in England.

---

[1] See, e.g., William Sherman, *John Dee: The Politics of Reading and Writing in the English Renaissance*, Massachusetts Studies in Early Medieval Culture (Amherst, MA: University of Massachusetts Press, 1995).

He owned at one time 3,000 books and 1,000 manuscripts, and had quite as good a claim to be the founder of a national library as Thomas Bodley or Robert Cotton.

The Dees were Welsh: John Dee's father was Chief Sewer to Henry VIII, later becoming a merchant. Educated at Chelmsford Grammar School and St John's College, Cambridge, John Dee was a Fellow of Trinity College. A tireless traveller, he went to the Netherlands to confer with astronomers and geographers such as Gemma Frisius and Gerardus Mercator; to Louvain and Paris to study (1548–50); to Switzerland and Italy (1562–4) for Conrad Gesner and Federigo Commandino; and twice to Poland (1563, 1583–4) for the Emperor Rudolf. Having been admitted to the Mercers' Company in 1555, Dee applied his geographical skills by advising on trading ventures.

Dee was charged with the offence of calculating royal nativities; but was able to persuade his examiner Bishop Bonner of his loyalty and orthodoxy— so convincingly that he became his chaplain. Within a few years another patron, Leicester, consulted him as to astrologically propitious days for Elizabeth's coronation. By 1565 Dee was wealthy enough to settle at Mortlake, assemble his growing library, and engage in alchemy. In 1570 came his 'Mathematical Preface' to an important edition of Euclid.

An advocate of imperial expansion in the New World, Dee may indeed have been the first to use the term 'British Empire'. He advised Martin Frobisher and George Peckham on the project of settling English Catholics in Norombega (Massachusetts and Maine), and for a time also advised on exploration of a possible north-west passage, until replaced by Sir Walter Ralegh. Dee's *General and Rare Memorials Pertaining to the Perfect Art of Navigation* was intended as part of a larger work (*The British Monarchy*) advocating a policy of strengthening England politically, economically, and as a naval power.

Frame

The pictorial title page is divided in diapason proportion. In the upper, smaller compartment, the title is framed by a band describing two horizontals with semicircular ends. At the L and R extremities, the cord forming the outer edge of the band is twisted to enclose the stems of two Tudor roses. At the top centre the royal arms, encircled by the Garter, are superimposed on the band. The lower compartment contains, within a square frame, an allegorical scene.

Tableau

In the sky at the extreme R, the *Tetragrammaton* or four-lettered name of God (YHWH) illuminates all: the sun with a face; the moon in its phases (full, crescent, and gibbous, with a face); and a cluster of stars. The ten stars between sun and moon are probably meant to indicate the constellation Delphinus (Dolphin). Ptolemy's *Almagest* and Hyginus' *Poetikon astronomikon* both catalogue Delphinus as formed by ten stars. The only other constellation of ten stars is Lyra. Either way, the stars allude mythologically to the rescue of Arion. After a last performance on his lyre, Arion was famously made to walk the plank by sea-robbers behaving much like pirates of the Elizabethan age.

Below the sun flies an angel, identified by a Hebrew scroll as the Archangel Michael. He carries a shield bearing the cross of Christ, and raises a wavy (perhaps fiery) sword. Below Michael, *Occasio* (Opportunity) with her long forelock stands precariously with one foot on the apex of a pyramid and the other on a rocky pinnacle. She carries a razor, a reminder that those who fail to seize her lock will find her occiput bald and elusive.

Beside Occasio is the ship ΕΥΡΩΠΗ (Europe), on which Queen Elizabeth (identified by a scroll) sits on a canopied throne, holding a cornucopia. Below her, Zeus in the guise of a bull carries off Europa: an allusion to her rape by Cretan pirates.[2] Piracy was common in Dee's time. The first part of the *General and Rare Memorials* is a plea (p. 53) for a 'pety-navy-royall', a task force of some sixty tall ships and smaller craft, to police the Channel and combat the pirates who infested the British seas. In 1563 these were known to number 400. Dee's proposal is for a tax levied on goods and rents throughout England. He cites the historical precedent of the Byzantine tax in defence of the Peloponnesian coast.

---

[2] Herodotus, *The Histories*, 1.23–4.

Towards the end of Dee's book he offers an explanation of the frontispiece, identifying the suppliant woman on the shore as a personification of *Res-Publica Britannica* (the British state), soliciting Elizabeth '(sitting at the helm of this Imperial Monarchy: or, rather, at the Helm of the Imperiall Ship, of the most parte of Christendome)'. Here Dee refers to the widespread ideal of Elizabeth as the just virgin of imperial reform. In fact, the ship of Europe is Dee's symbol of *renovatio*.[3] The suppliant's plea is that a 'well-equipped force' may be raised, to give security, but make her subjects partakers of public 'commodities innumerable' (symbolized in the cornucopia of advantages) (p. 53).

To the L of the European ship is a walled town on which Occasion precariously stands: the opportunity to realize the country's aspiration to security. It is identified by a scroll as 'the citadel of security'.

Below the citadel and to the L is a ship flying the British ensign (four bands as distinct from the Netherlands' three and Flushing's five). It is the answer to the pirate ships above L, against which Michael raises his sword. A land force patrols the coast with torches. It consists of swordsmen and musketeers (not harquebuses, since they have no tripods), and is led by a mounted captain with a lance. All wear 'Spanish morions', a type of helmet common at the time throughout Europe. Some of the privateers are English, shown being 'constrained to come home' by the coastguard, whether by force or financial incentives (p. 6). The Petty Navy, Dee argues, would attract foreign contributions. The marine police would also commandeer corn and keep it in one or another of the storehouses at their base towns—a measure against hoarding and the counterfeit dearth symbolized by the inverted wheat and the half skull (p. 39).

Corbett and Lightbown see the citadel of security on a mountainous headland as alluding to Mistra in the Peloponnese, the city that offered a historical precedent for the success of a naval force and strings of fortresses. Dee reprints addresses by Gemistus Pletho. But the architecture of the citadel hardly supports so specific an allusion, as a glance at Braun and Hogenberg's *Cities of the World* shows. Nor is the use of Greek any more conclusive: it is part of Dee's fondness for esoteric symbols.

---

[3] See Frances Yates, *Astraea: The Imperial Theme in the Sixteenth Century* (London: Routledge & Kegan Paul, 1975), 123 and 29–87 *passim*.

Inscriptions

Round the band in the upper compartment a Latin motto is inscribed: PLVRA LATENT QVAM PATENT ('more things are hidden than obvious'; a common saying in the Paracelsian tradition). In the Preface to *The Jewell House of Art and Nature* (1594), Sir Hugh Platt writes of 'that old envied sentence (PLVRA LATENT QVAM PATENT), being written in capitall letters, by the hande of Nature'.

Within the band is the title: GENERAL AND RARE MEMORIALS PERTAINING TO THE PERFECT ARTE OF NAVIGATION: ANNEXED TO THE PARADOXAL COMPASS, IN PLAYNE: NOW FIRST PUBLISHED: 24 YERES, AFTER THE FIRST INVENTION THEREOF. The 'paradoxal compass', commissioned from Dee for the Muscovy Company master pilots, was so called in reference to three types of course: horizontal, paradoxal, and on a great circle. Paradoxal sailing described a spiral when the same course was followed continuously.[4]

Round the border of the lower compartment, in Greek, a caption to the frontispiece reads ΙΕΡΟΓΛΥΦΙΚΟΝ ΒΡΥΤΑΝΙΚΟΝ ('a hieroglyph of Britain'). Within the frontispiece itself are two scrolls, discussed above, under *tableau*: the suppliant begs for Στολος εξωπλισμενος ('a well-equipped force') and the fortified town is identified as το της ασφαλειας φρουριον ('the citadel of security').

Chronogram

In the corners of the lower compartment are roundels each containing a Greek numeral. Of these, the upper L has α with a slant line, that is, 1,000; while the upper R has φ, an error for φ with a slant line, that is, 500. The lower L roundel has ο, again in error for ό, that is, 70. Finally, the lower R roundel has ς with the upper curve correctly extended into a horizontal line, the symbol for 6. In sum, the symbols indicate 1576, the year of publication. Dee had taught Greek at Cambridge, so the errors are unlikely to be his. The printer

---

[4] See *OED*, s.v. *Paradoxal* a.

John Daye had a high standard of correctness, and employed compositors experienced in setting Greek; but in the sixteenth century such errors often escaped proofreaders.[5]

Faulty as it is, the chronogram is very early for an English book: it may have been influential in establishing the convention.[6]

Printer

John Daye (1521/2–84) may have begun work as a servant of the printer Thomas Raynalde. In 1546 he was freed of the London Stringers' [bowstring-makers] Company, one of a group buying their City freedom.[7] Very soon he transferred to the Stationers' Company, and set up as a printer, first at the sign of the Resurrection, and from 1549 at the gatehouse of Aldergate. Working first with William Serres and others of the Protestant book trade, he kept up a steady stream of small-format books with an evangelical tendency, bringing to the English market significant works of continental Protestantism by John Calvin, Herman von Wied, and others.

During the reign of Edward VI Daye was involved in printing as many as 130 works. But under the Marian regime Day was in difficulties. He seems to have been involved in the clandestine publication of Protestant tracts, perhaps using the pseudonym of Michael Wood of Rouen. In October 1554 he was arrested and briefly imprisoned. But with Elizabeth's accession he resumed his former career. He obtained a privilege to print William Cunningham's *The Cosmographical Glasse* (1559), also the *ABC with Little Catechism* and Sternhold and Hopkins's best-selling English psalter. These, together with editions of Becon and Tyndale, made him rich and envied, much in need of the protection of his patron, Robert Dudley, earl of Leicester.

Later, Daye took on larger ventures, notably John Foxe's 1,800-page *Book of Martyrs* (1563). This immense work made complex demands on the printer, having different typefaces, marginalia, columns, and new woodcut

[5] See Anthony Grafton, *The Culture of Correction in Renaissance Europe*, Panizzi Lecture, 2009 (London: British Library, 2011), 78–142 *passim*.

[6] See Introduction: Chronograms.

[7] See Peter W. M. Blayney, *The Stationers' Company and the Printers of London 1501–1557*, 2 vols (Cambridge: Cambridge University Press, 2013), i. 27–8.

illustrations. For the second edition of 1,250 copies (1570), Day used three presses and employed (as throughout his career) skilled workmen from the Netherlands. The project probably involved an investment of some £1,000; but it was highly successful, and made both his reputation and his fortune.

Daye's work was characterized by professional assurance and typographic accomplishment. His pre-eminence throughout his career can be attributed in part to his close connections with continental printing houses and his extensive use of foreign expertise. In particular, his workmen had experience in setting Greek type. He was an obvious choice as official printer to the City authorities. But he also diversified and took on important specialized projects. Two of these stand out. For his friend Matthew Parker he published Aelfric's *Testimonie of Antiquity* (1566), a work that called for the casting of Anglo-Saxon letters. And, most renowned of all, he published an English translation of Euclid's *Elements of Geometry* (1570), a deluxe folio with pop-up diagrams, for which Dee wrote the famous 'Mathematical Preface'.[8]

Designer

A preliminary drawing of the frontispiece is extant, among the papers of Elias Ashmole.[9] Although this differs in minor ways from the printed frontispiece, it establishes that the design is almost certainly Dee's. The fact that the drawing has no frame round the title may suggest that John Daye had a hand in finalizing the layout.

The esoteric character of Dee's design is found in several of his other works, notably the *Monas Hieroglyphica* (Antwerp, 1564). He was strongly drawn to the symbols of Renaissance Hermeticism, and regarded himself as a magus.[10]

---

[8] See Allen Debus, *The English Paracelsians* (New York: Watts, 1966).

[9] Bodley, Ashmole MS 1789. See Peter J. French, *John Dee: The World of an Elizabethan Magus* (London: Routledge & Kegan Paul, 1972; New York: Dorset, 1989), pl. 14.

[10] See C. H. Josten, 'A Translation of John Dee's *Monas hieroglyphicum* (Antwerp, 1564)', *Ambix*, 12 (1964), 83–221; French, *John Dee*, esp. ch. 4.

ORLANDO

FVRIOSO

IN ENGLISH

HEROICAL VERSE, BY

IOHN HARINGTŌ

Principibus placuisse viris non vltima laus est.

Horace

John Harington
ORLANDO FURIOSO IN ENGLISH HEROICAL VERSE (1591)

S ir John Harington's magnificent *Orlando furioso* translation has been called 'the most ambitious [English] book illustrated with metal plates in the [sixteenth] century.[1] It must certainly have been very expensive to produce. Probably Harington himself financed the edition, or at least guaranteed it. He was rightly proud of his achievement, as the 'Advertisement to the Reader' suggests:

As for the pictures, they are all cut in brasse [copper] and most of them by the best workmen in that kinde that have bene in this land this many years; yet I will not

---

[1] Alfred William Pollard, *Early Illustrated Books* (London: Kegan Paul, Trench, Trübner, 1893), 249. See Ludovico Ariosto, *Ludovico Ariosto's* Orlando Furioso *Translated into English Heroical Verse by Sir John Harington (1591)*, ed. Robert McNulty (Oxford: Clarendon Press, 1972), p. xlvii.

praise them too much, because I gave direction for their making, and in regard thereof I may be thought partiall, but this I may truely say, that (for mine owne part) I have not seene anie made in England better nor (in deede) anie of this kinde in any booke

—except in Hugh Broughton's *Concent of Scripture* (1588–90), which had copper engravings by William Rogers—

as for other books that I have seen in this realme, either in Latin or English, with pictures, as Livy, Gesner, Alciats emblems [...] and (in our tong) Whitneys excellent Emblems, yet all their figures are cut in wood and none in metal, and in that respect inferior to these, at least (by the old proverbe) the more cost, the more worship.[2]

He describes the full-page plates preceding each canto and summarizes their contents as serving the purpose of memory prompts. They are closely modelled on the superb plates in Francesco de Franceschi's Ariosto of 1584. For that, Girolamo Porro (fl. 1567–99) had brilliantly redrawn the plates and redone the title page, replacing earlier caryatids with mythological figures (Fig. 13).[3] Thomas Cockson and the other English artists imitating Porro's plates drew less well and were less meticulous in captioning. But Harington's success was real: he had not only brought copper engraving to England, but done so in a translation that was to prove seminal.

Tableau

In de' Franceschi's 1584 title page Porro introduced statues of Mars (L) and Venus with Cupid (R), to represent the subjects referred to in Ariosto's opening *propositio*, 'Le donne, i cavallier, l'armi, gli amori | Le cortesie, l'audaci imprese io canto' ('Of Dames, of Knights, of armes, of loves delight, | Of curtesies, of high attempts I speake').

---

[2] *Ariosto's* Orlando Furioso, ed. McNulty, 17.
[3] On Porro, see Michael Bury, *The Print in Italy 1550–1620* (London: British Museum, 2001), 231.

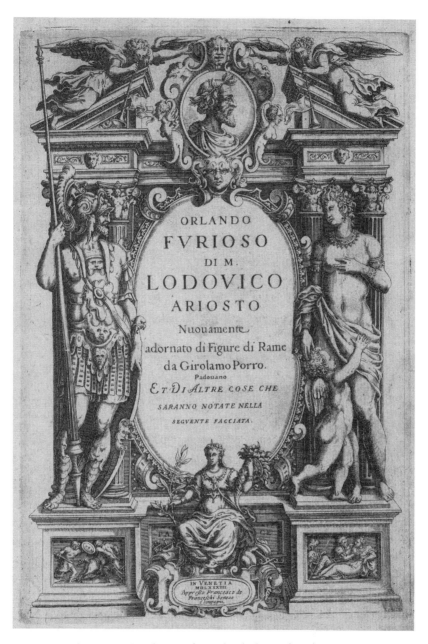

Fig. 13. Girolamo Porro's title page for *Orlando furioso* (1584). Douce A Subt. 34, Title Page. Courtesy of the Bodleian Libraries, The University of Oxford.

The 1591 edition of Harington's translation retained much of Porro's title page. The portrait of Ariosto still appears in the upper medallion, flanked by *Famae* (recognizable from their trumpets); the title is still flanked by Mars (L) and Venus and Cupid (R). And there are still bas-reliefs representing scenes of war and love. But the figure of Peace with olive branch and cornucopia is gone, replaced by a portrait of Harington. De' Franceschi's title page followed a familiar scheme of 'architecture' and medallions. (His upper medallion showed Ariosto; his lower, Peace.) Harington's title page follows much of this. His upper medallion shows Ariosto in classical garb, within an oval frame inset within a strapwork cartouche. All this occupies the centre of a broken pediment, on which double *Famae* still recline.

Instead of Peace, however, the lower medallion now contains a portrait of Harington. (This compositional format, with author portrait above and translator below, was becoming a standard one.) Harington is portrayed behind a table; on it rests an open watch displaying the Harington arms (a fret, or true-lover's knot) engraved inside its cover.[4]

Inscriptions

The frame of Ariosto's portrait now bears an inscription: IL DIVINO LUDOVICO ARIOSTO. Below this, a cartouche surrounds the book's title, ORLANDO FVRIOSO IN ENGLISH HEROICAL VERSE, BY IOHN HARINGTON, together with an ambiguous quotation from Horace *Epistles* 1.17.35, PRINCIPIBUS PLACUISSE VIRIS NON VLTIMA LAVS EST. H. R. Fairclough, missing the point, translates: 'Yet to have won favour with the foremost men is not the lowest glory'; Gerard Kilroy, more convincingly, has: 'The greatest praise does not come from having pleased princes.'[5] The verse immediately preceding—'To achieve great deeds and to display captive foemen to one's fellow citizens is to touch the throne of Jove and to scale the skies'—alludes to Augustus' triumphal career.

---

[4] The Harrington knot or fret consists of two long pieces in saltire, extending to the extremities of the field and interlaced with a mascle or perforated lozenge; see Charles Norton Elvin, *A Dictionary of Heraldry* (1889), pls 43.9 and 5.19.

[5] Gerard Kilroy, *The Epigrams of Sir John Harington* (Ashgate, 2009), 15.

The lower medallion with the translator's portrait bears two further inscriptions. The first gives Harington's birthday and age as PRIMO AUGUSTI ANNO DOMINI 1591 AETAS 50 ('on the first of August, 1591, aged 30'). The gratuitous precision of the date may be intended to glance at Elizabeth as a second Augustus.[6] The other inscription on the portrait's oval frame reads IL TEMPO PASSA ('time passes').[7] Since Harington is portrayed with a watch, this inscription suggests an emblem motto often accompanying a picture of a timepiece.[8]

Yet another inscription occupies a banderole or speech bubble issuing from the mouth of the spaniel couchant on the tiled floor. By overlapping the portrait, the banderole identifies the spaniel with his master as a *fictio* of Harington himself. The banderole inscription, FIN CHE VENGA, is a quotation from *Orlando furioso*, 41.30.5–8, describing Olivero's crest:

> Un can d'argento aver vuole Oliviero,
> Ce giaccia, e che las lassa abbia sul dosso
> Con un motto che dica: Fin che vegna […]

—translated by Harington as:

> His cosin had a Lyme hound argent bright,
> His Lyme [leash] layd on his backe, he couching downe;
> The word or Mot was this: untill he commeth;
> The rest was rich and such as him becommeth […][9]

Ariosto's commentators explain that Olivero awaits an occasion of giving proof of his valour in the Christian cause; and Harington's own Allusion note begins similarly:

---

[6] Harington was baptized on 4 August 1561.

[7] See Virgil, *Georgics* 3.284, sed fugit interea, fugit inreperabile *Tempus*; ODEP, s.v. *Time flies*; Morris Palmer Tilley, *A Dictionary of the Proverbs in England in the Sixteenth and Seventeenth Centuries* (Ann Arbor, MI: University of Michigan Press, 1950), T 327, 'Time flees away without delay (has wings)'.

[8] See, e. g., Thomas Combe, *The Theatre of Fine Devices* (1614), 68, 71; John Hall, *Emblems with Elegant Figures* (1658), 104; George Wither, *A Collection of Emblems* (1635), 212, 235, 257, 'time is always from thee flying'; Geoffrey Whitney, *A Choice of Emblems* (Leiden, 1586), 199.

[9] *Ariosto's* Orlando Furioso, ed. McNulty, 480.

as the Spaniell or hound that is at commaundement waiteth till the fowle or deare be stricken and then boldly leapeth into the water or draweth after it by land, so he being yet a young man waited for an occasion to shew his value, which being come, he would no longer couch but shew the same.

But then Harington applies the device to himself:

My selfe have chosen this of Olivero for my owne, partly liking the modestie thereof, partly (for I am not ashamed to confesse it) because I fancie the Spaniell so much whose picture is in the devise, and if anie make merie at it (as I doubt not but some will) I shall not be sorie for it, for one end of my travel in this worke is to make my frends merie, and besides I can alleage many examples of wise men and some verie great men that have not onely taken pictures but built cities in remembrance of serviceable beasts.[10]

Harington called his spaniel Bungay after Friar Bungay, the famous conjuror in Edward IV's time. The same 'jolly frier' Bungay is Friar Bacon's assistant in Robert Greene's *Frier Bacon and Frier Bongay* (1594), lines 629–31. Harington's spaniel is similarly given to pretty pranks. The banderole motto UNTILL HE COMMETH may simply refer to the dog's patient waiting to be of service, a figure of Harington's holding himself ready for 'occasion to show his worth' in political service. But Harington's jests often conceal deeper meanings. 'Until he comes' has an apocalyptic ring, as in 1 Cor. 4: 5, 'judge nothing before the time, until the Lord come, who both will bring to light the hidden things of darkness, and will make manifest the counsel of the hearts: and then shall every man have praise of God'.

Kilroy notes that at least one of Harington's contemporaries appreciated something of Bungay's significance. Sir John Davies mentions, among examples of animals better known than their masters, 'Lepidus his printed dog'.[11] This has been taken as criticizing the inappropriateness of putting a dog on a title page; but in Kilroy's view Harington's friend Davies knew he was 'using Bungey to present himself as an unthreatening and avuncular figure'.[12]

---

[10] *Ariosto's* Orlando Furioso, 480.

[11] Sir John Davies, Epigram 48, 'Ad Musam'.

[12] Kilroy, *The Epigrams*, 76; Sir John Harington, *Nugae Antiquae: Being a Miscellaneous Collection of Original Papers in Prose and Verse*, ed. Thomas Park, 2 vols (1804), i. 1. 380–4.

Publication

Ambitious as Richard Field's 1591 edition was, he also printed a large-paper issue of presentation copies, some with coloured title page and plates. In several presentation copies, such as that for Lord Burghley, the text is enclosed throughout with hand-ruled frames; and in Lady Arabella Stuart's copy the title page, colophon, plates, initial letters of the cantos, and printer's ornaments, are hand-coloured.[13] Harington clearly wanted his translation to have some of the personal qualities of a manuscript book. This preference also shows in later publications, which include eight manuscript books.[14] This was not so old-fashioned as it may appear: manuscript publication continued well into the seventeenth century,[15] and continues to this day in Christmas books distributed privately.

The personalized, semi-manuscript format was not only an aesthetic preference of Harington. Like modern samizdat publication, it tried to escape the institutional organization of printed publication on which control of the press by licensing authorities depended. In effect, Harington's *Orlando Furioso* had variant texts assigned to distinct readerships. Some versions contained subversive satire that would hardly have passed the licensing authorities.[16] On the other hand, a presentation copy made for Lady Rogers, Harington's mother-in-law, and his wife, Mary, contains fifty-two epigrams in manuscript bound together with the *Orlando furioso* translation.[17] In the same way, Harington personalized presentation copies of *Metamorphosis of Ajax*.[18] Harington's mode of publication contrasts sharply with the impersonal classicism of Jonson.

Printer

Richard Field or Feild (1561–1624), a Stratford man apprenticed to George Bishop, served under the Huguenot Thomas Vautrollier, Printer to King

[13] See Kilroy, *The Epigrams*, 15.

[14] Ibid. 16.

[15] See Harold Love, *Scribal Publication in Seventeenth-Century England* (Oxford: Clarendon Press, 1993).

[16] See Kilroy, *The Epigrams*, 16–19.

[17] Ibid. 70.

[18] Ibid 66 n. 56. On a presentation copy for Queen Elizabeth, see *Ariosto's* Orlando Furioso, ed. McNulty, l.

James VI. Made free of the Stationers' Company in 1587, Field inherited Vautrollier's business, becoming one of the leading stationers in London at the young age of 27. He kept up Vautrollier's contacts with King James, Burleigh, and other English courtiers; publishing such high-profile works as Puttenham's *The Arte of English Poesie* (1589), North's translation of Plutarch's *Lives* (1595, 1603), Spenser's *The Faerie Queene* (1596), and Sidney's *Arcadia* (1598). He served as Master of the Stationers' Company in 1619 and 1622.[19]

Designer

From two manuscripts (Bodl., MS Rawlinson poet. 125 and BL, Add. MS 18920) we know that Harington himself took a hand in designing the title page of *Orlando furioso*. At first he seems to have had in mind a more elaborate format than that of the 1591 edition. But the experienced Field knew a more economical plan, and hired a beginner, Thomas Cockson or Coxon (bap. 1569, d. before 1641?) to copy much of Porro's 1584 title page. Cockson was apprenticed to William Rogers in 1584 but became a Freeman of the Goldsmiths' Company only in 1598. Much of his work was engraved portraits, which made him an intelligible choice for Harington's 1591 title page with its portraits of poet and translator. Cockson's engraving style (in this his first work for the book trade) is characterized by Strutt as done 'entirely with the graver, in a neat, stiff style, which seems to prove, that he had much more industry than genius'.[20]

Harington and Field together probably decided to substitute the translator's portrait for Porro's figure of Peace. But Harington himself was certainly responsible for the inscriptions, and for introducing the spaniel Bungay.

---

[19] See A. E. M. Kirkwood, 'Richard Field, Printer, 1589–1624', *Library*, 4th ser., 12 (1931–2), 1–39; *Ariosto's* Orlando Furioso, ed. McNulty, pp. xli–xlii; *ODNB*.

[20] See Arthur Hind, *Engraving in England in the Sixteenth and Seventeenth Centuries*, i. *The Tudor Period* (Cambridge: Cambridge University Press, 1952), 239–57; Joseph Strutt, *A Biographical Dictionary* [...] *of* [...] *Engravers*, 2 vols (1785–6).

Harington's translation had two early editions, in 1591 and 1607. In a bibliographical tour de force, Randall McLeod has pursued the many consequences of using the same paper stock to support both letterpress and engraving—the differential broadening of sheets, with resultant folding, tearing, and slicing.[21]

---

[21] Randall McLeod, 'The Fog of arr', *Leia*, 26 (2013), 163–247. See also Simon Cauchi, 'The "Setting Foorth" of Harington's Ariosto', *Studies in Bibliography*, 36 (1983), 137–68.

POLY-OLBION

GREAT BRITAINE

By
Michaell Drayton
Esqr:

London printed for M. Lownes. I. Browne. I. Helme. I. Busbie.

Michael Drayton
POLY-OLBION
1612, 1622

UPON THE *FRONTISPICE*

Through a Triumphant arch, see Albion plas't,
In Happy site, in Neptunes armes embras't
In Power and Plenty, on hir Cleevy [cliffy] Throne
Circled with Natures Ghirlands, being alone
Stil'd th'Oceans Island. On the columns been
(As Trophies raiz'd) what Princes Time hath seene
Ambitious of her. In hir youger years,
Vast Earth-bred Giants woo'd her: but, who bears
In Golden field the Lion passant red,
Aeneas Nephew (Brute) them conquered.
Next, Laureat Caesar, as a Philtre, brings,
On's shield, his Grandame Venus: Him hir Kings
Withstood. At length, the Roman, by long sute,

Gain'd her (most Part) from th'ancient race of Brute.
Divors'd from Him, the Saxon sable Horse,
Borne by sterne Hengist, wins her: but, through force
Garding the Norman *Leopards bath'd in Gules*,
She chang'd hir Love to Him, whose Line yet rules.[1]

This masterpiece of river georgic celebrates the land in terms of its rivers. In this, it resembles William Camden's *Britannia* (1586). Graham Parry goes so far as to describe *Poly-Olbion* as '*Britannia* versified'.[2] Drayton's notes show him using *Britannia* from 1597 on; although he consulted the libraries of John Selden and Robert Cotton as well as Camden's.[3]

Layout

The pictorial title page shows several features comparable with the frontispiece of Camden's 1607 *Britannia*. Both use the common layout of two medallions and a tableau of figures. The *Poly-Olbion* frontispiece shows a triumphal arch springing from square pilasters that rest on a stepped plinth decorated with scallops. As usual with show architecture in books, the plinth closes off entry through the arch: it primarily exists to display the title and the figure of Albion. In front of each pilaster is a round column—Doric, as the georgic genre and the theme of antiquity required. These columns support, instead of an entablature, pedestals for the upper two of the tableau figures. The triumphal arch is set in an arcade, through the lesser arches of which a maritime vista appears. This arcade rests on the plinth, and in turn supports a balustrade. The triumphal arch, however, is surmounted by round crenellations interrupted at the centre by a scalloped niche finished with a segmental coping and flanked by obelisks. Well behind the crenellations rises

[1] Probably by John Selden, or Selden and Drayton together.
[2] See Graham Parry, 'Ancient Britons and Early Stuarts', in Robin Headlam Wells, Glenn Burgess, and Rowland Wymer (eds), *Neo-Historicism: Studies in Renaissance Literature, History and Politics* (Cambridge: D. S. Brewer, 2000), 161.
[3] Bernard H. Newdigate, *Michael Drayton and his Circle* (Oxford: Blackwell for the Shakespeare Head Press, 1961), 24, 93–4.

a small structure (temple or banqueting house) with a fluted ogival roof on Doric columns. This structure has no visible means of support.

Suspended from the obelisks is a cartouche, which in turn supports a marine swag of crabs, corals, scallops, sea potatoes, winkles, limpets, and necklace shells—'the delicacies of the Sea', as Song XX has it:

> Of Currall of each kind, the blacke, the red, the white;
> With many sundry shels, the Scallop large, and faire;
> The Cockle small and round, the Periwinkle spare,
> The Oyster, wherein oft the pearle is found to breed,
> The Mussell, which retaines that daintie Orient seed:
> In Chaines and Bracelets made, with linkes of sundry twists [...]
> (*Poly-Olbion*, Song XX, lines 104–9)

Title

The upper cartouche frames the title, POLY-OLBION. *Olbion* is a variant of *Albion*, the ancient Greek name for Britain. *Poly-* suggests 'Variety' or 'Profusion Britain'. But the title may also suggest Greek *Polyolbos*, 'Rich in belongings'; and may even play on 'all be one'.[4] In short, wordplay conflates the name of Britain with description of the abundant resources emblemized in Albion's cornucopia. Behind these suggestions is Camden's section on 'The Name of Britain', where he cites 'the Coins of Antoninus Pius and Severus [where] Britain is figured sitting upon Rocks, in a womans habit'.[5] Drayton's frontispieces of 1612 and 1622, like that of Camden's 1607 *Britannia*, were engraved by William Hole.

At some time between 1628 and 1633, a change to the title *Poly-Olbion* may have been considered. In a unique copy of the third issue of part I bound with part II, on the recto of the first leaf (normally blank), has been printed, in

---

[4] Alexander Gardyne's wordplay in *A Garden of Grave and Godlie Flowres* (1609); see Anne Lake Prescott, *ODNB*.

[5] Camden, *Britannia*, trans. E. Gibson (London, 1695), col. xxvii; see Parry, 'Ancient Britons', 161; *The Golden Age Restored: The Culture of the Stuart Court, 1603–42* (Manchester: Manchester University Press, 1981), 82.

large capitals, the title THE | FAERIE | LAND, within a frame of printer's ornaments which belonged to John Litchfield, printer to the University of Oxford 1605–35. On the verso of this first leaf of part I, above the first line ('Vpon the *Frontispice*'), has been printed 'The FAERIE LAND'. This variant may have been planned as part of an attempt to make more attractive a book that was not selling well.[6]

On the frontispiece of *Poly-Olbion*, below the figure of Albion, is a second inscription, GREAT BRITAINE, overprinted on the rocks. The lower cartouche frames a third inscription: 'By Michaell Drayton Esqur.' Finally, on the ground below the plinth is the imprint: 'London printed for M. Lownes, I. Browne, I. Helme, I. Busbie. Ingraven by W. Hole.'

Tableau

By far the largest of the five allegorical figures is Albion, figured as a young woman with the loose hair of an unmarried girl. Sidney Colvin thought Albion's legs 'stumpy'; but Anne Lake Prescott rightly sees her as 'positioned so as to give her the same shape as her nation'.[7] Celebrated by a winged Fame with a trumpet and crowned with a laurel wreath by two more putti, Albion sits on the rocks of Great Britain, amidst a sea swarming with whales, sea monsters, and ships. In her R hand she holds a sceptre tipped with a fleur-de-lis like the French royal sceptre, and in the crook of her L arm lies a cornucopia. Her cloak, decorated with a topographical map of her country, leaves her L breast exposed. These attributes all emblemize aspects of Honour, the reward of virtue, as explained in Cesare Ripa's *Iconologia* (1611): 'a staff, cornucopia, and laurel crown signify the three main occasions for which men are customarily honoured.' Vitellio's medal represents Honour as 'a young woman with a staff in her right hand and a cornucopia in her left, with her breasts half exposed; showing that she can defend her honour with force, and preserve her purity'.[8] Albion's sceptre tipped with a fleur-de-lis had a

---

[6] See Bent Juel-Jensen, 'An Oxford Variant of Drayton's *Polyolbion*', *Library*, 5th ser., 16 (1961), 52–4.

[7] Newdigate, *Drayton*, 230; *ODNB*.

[8] Ripa, *Iconologia* (Padua, 1611; facsimile edn, New York and London: Garland, 1976), 219–20.

precedent in coins struck for King Canute (available to Hole in engravings that he probably also used for his Roman emperor). Canute's sub-imperial sceptre carries implications of England's European status.[9] Although Calais was lost in 1558, England's claims to sovereignty over France were not abandoned until the Peace of Amiens in 1802.

Albion wears a triple necklace of pearls and drop earrings of pearl, in allusion to the ancient harvesting of pearls from British rivers: 'Irt, of all the rest, though small, the richest Girle, | Her costly bosom strew'd with precious Orient Pearle, | Bred in her shining Shels [...]' (*Poly-Olbion*, Song XXX, lines 115–17). In this Drayton follows Camden, who tells how the 'shell-fish [...] bring forth Pearls, or (to use the Poet's name) *Shell-berries*. These the Inhabitants gather up at low water; and the Jewellers buy them of the poor people for a trifle, and sell them at a good price.'[10] Camden in turn cites Pliny, *Natural History* 9.50.7: 'small pearls of poor colour grow in Britain [...] the late lamented Julius desired it to be known that the breast-plate that he dedicated to Venus Genetrix in her temple was made of British pearls.'[11]

The other four principal figures represent conquerors of Britain and their dynasties: 'What Princes Time hath seene | Ambitious of her':[12] British, upper L; Roman, upper R; Saxon, lower L; Norman, lower R. The first conqueror is Trojan Brut, a long-haired youth wearing coat armour of 1400, a square-necked surcoat, laced boots, and a soft cap. His L hand rests on the pommel of a straight sword hanging from his belt, and suspended from his R arm is a shield bearing a lion passant. Following Geoffrey of Monmouth, Matthew of Paris, Higden's *Polychronicon*, Robert Wace's *Roman de Brut*, and Layamon's *Brut*, Drayton accepts their myth of national origin, whereby Brut gave his name to the British ancestors of the Welsh. In the sixteenth century, the myth was discredited by historians—Camden, for example, and Polydore Vergil. Selden was sceptical too: his preface refers to the tradition as 'much controverted and by Cambro-Britons [Welsh] still maintained,

---

[9] See L. O. Lagerqvist and R. H. M. Dolley, 'The Problem of the "Fleur-de-Lis" Sceptre on the Sigtuna Coins of Cnut', *British Numismatic Journal*, 30 (1960), 23.
[10] Camden, *Britannia* (1695), col. 820.
[11] Pliny, *Natural History*, trans. H. Rackham (London: Folio Society, 2012), 2.88.
[12] See 'Upon the Frontispice'.

touching the Troyan Brute'. He himself countenances it only 'as an Advocate for the Muse'. For Brut's armorial charge, Drayton or Selden relies on John Harding's *Chronicle* (1543), ch. 12: 'He bare of goules two lyons of golde | Countre Rampant with golde onely crowned | Which kynges of Troy n battail bare [...]'. Selden owned manuscripts of the fifteenth-century herald Nicholas Upton, which gave Brut's arms as 'a lion passant gules'.

The second conqueror, upper R, is a laureate Roman emperor wearing *lorica*, *zoma*, and cloak, and holding a staff or spear and a sword. His shield, suspended from the cartouche, bears a semi-nude Venus holding up a flaming heart. (The Julian house claimed descent from Venus through Aeneas her son.) Drayton—or Selden—justifies the charge in a marginal note to 'Upon the Frontispice'. Informed by the engravings in such authorities as Hubert Goltz or Guillaume De Choul, he 'took Venus proper to him, for that the stamp of hir face [...] in his Coins is frequent'. Drayton—and probably also Hole—took the head of Caesar from an ancient medal or coin, engraved in a similar source.[13] The flaming heart held by Venus was a common emblem: it usually signified that 'man's heart aspires to God but is oppressed by sin. God lifts it to heaven;'[14] but here the association with Aeneas may be the main idea.

The bearded third conqueror (lower L), Hengist, wears a helmet like a kettle-hat or morion, scale or chain mail, a skirt, and turned-down thigh boots. In his R hand he holds a strange weapon, which has been identified as a *spetum* (a pole weapon of the thirteenth century, 6–8 feet long with a three-pointed metal head), although its cross-bar suggests rather a shortened boar-spear. Perhaps Hole was thinking of the tournament puncheon-staff used in foot combats. But the various armours in the tableau have little if any historical foundation: Hole may well have based them on what he had seen in pageants or stage plays or prints. Hengist's shield bears 'the Saxon sable Horse'; Horse, as Drayton and Selden explain, is the meaning of *Hengist*. His

---

[13] Hubert Golz, *Thesaurus antiquariae huberrimus, ex antiquis tam numismatum quam marmorum inscriptionibus* [...] (Antwerp, 1579).

[14] Epigram to H.A. [Henry Hawkins], *The Devout Heart* (Rouen, 1634), 14, 'The Consecration of the Heart'. Cf. Mario Praz, *Studies in Seventeenth-Century Imagery*, 2nd enlarged edn (Rome: Edizioni di Storia e Letteratura, 1964), 130, 152; *The Flaming Heart* (New York: Doubleday, 1958), 204–63.

skirt resembles that of the representative Saxon in the frontispiece of John Speed's *History of Great Britaine* (1611), where a shield bears the charge of a horse.

The fourth (lower R) figure is William the Conqueror, wearing the St Edward's crown traditional since Edward the Confessor, but without the fleurs-de-lis or trefoils on the circlet. William's R hand holds a drawn sword, while his L arm supports a shield bearing the arms of England (three leopards—'the Norman leopards bath'd in Gules', as Drayton and Selden's note has it[15]). On the authority of Matthew Paris, Selden's commentary on Song XI specifies the earlier arms of England as three leopards passant. Hole's engraving shows two of the three, uniformly spotted. The date is too early for his hatching to indicate any particular tincture.

Stationers

The complicated publishing history of *Poly-olbion* is partly obscure. In or before 1612, the first eighteen songs (part I) were printed; the last twelve songs (part II) were printed ten years later; and the titles were printed separately, in 1613 and 1622. In the preface to part II, Drayton complains that 'some of the Stationers, that had the Selling of the first part of this Poeme, because it went not so fast away in the Sale, as some of their beastly and abominable Trash [...] have either despightfully left out, or at least carelessely neglected the Epistles to the Readers'. These same stationers—Matthew Lownes, John Browne, John Helme, and John Busbie—published part I in 1612 but refused to touch part II. In 1619, Drayton wrote to Drummond of Hawthornden that he had written twelve more songs, but that 'the Booksellers and I are in terms [negotiating]: They are a Company of base Knaves, whom I both scorn and kick at.' Drayton considered moving to an Edinburgh stationer, but eventually persuaded a new consortium of London stationers (John Marriott, John Grismand, and Thomas Dewe) to publish part II.

---

[15] Commentary to Song XI, in Michael Drayton, *The Works*, ed. J. William Hebel, 5 vols (Oxford: Shakespeare Head Press, 1931–41), iv. 231–2.

Printer

Humphrey Lownes entered part I in the Stationers' Register on 2 February 1612, and printed it in the same year. It included 'Upon the Frontispice' facing Hole's frontispiece or title page. In 1613 the sheets of *Poly-olbion* were reissued: a printed title page now followed Hole's engraved frontispiece. In 1622, a third issue of part I was published, together with the first edition of part II. A letterpress title with the names of the new publishers now followed the engraved frontispiece. Selden did not contribute a commentary to part II.

Patrons

Prince Henry paid Drayton an annuity of £10 for *Poly-olbion*. After Henry's death in 1612, Prince Charles probably continued to pay this annuity.

Engraver

The frontispiece—and the portrait of Prince Henry—were engraved by William Hole or Holle (d. 1624). Hole was possibly a pupil of William Rogers: unlike most English engravers, he was influenced by French rather than Netherlandish engravers. He was a specialist in lettering; by comparison, his figurative plates were crude. But he did many portraits, and was on friendly terms with many of the foremost Jacobean poets and writers. His best work was for the Mint, where he engraved coin dies.

Designers

Probably William Hole and Drayton himself were the designers, perhaps with advice from Selden.

THE
WORKES
OF
Beniamin Jonson

— *neque, me vt miretur turba,*
laboro:
Contentus paucis lectoribus.

Imprinted at
London, by
Will Stansby

Ben Jonson
THE WORKES
1616

It was not unknown, before Jonson, to use the title 'Works': Nicholas Breton had published *The Workes of a young wyt* in 1577. But it was very unusual for a poet to publish a collected edition in his own lifetime, and even more unusual for stage plays to be published as 'Works'. Although *The Workes of Beniamin Jonson* (1616) include two collections of poems, it was the nine plays, seventeen masques, and other court entertainments that attracted comment at the time. From Sir John Suckling, for example:

> *To Mr Ben Jonson demanding the reason why he called his plays 'works'*
> Pray tell me, Ben, where doth the mystery lurk,
> What others call a play you call a work.

> *Thus answered by a friend in Mr Jonson's defence*
> The author's friend thus for the author says,
> Ben's plays are works, when other's works are plays.

The first that broke silence was good old Ben,
Prepar'd before with Canary wine,
And he told them plainly he deserv'd the Bayes,
For his were call'd Works, where others were but Plaies; [1]

('A Sessions of the Poets', stanza 3)

Jonson himself may in part have sensed the incongruity of calling plays works. At any rate, he paid less attention to correcting proofs of his plays than his poems. James Riddell convincingly relates the printing history of the 1616 *Workes* to this, and to Jonson's higher regard for the epigrams as 'the ripest of my studies'.[2]

Layout

At first glance the title page, engraved by William Hole, may seem architectural. But if it were, what building type would it exemplify? Stephen Orgel suggests, a triumphal arch;[3] but there is no such arch here, only a façade. The layout is more like a pegme or pageant frame using architectural elements decoratively.[4] So the figures flanking the title stand on pedestals improvised from corbels, capitals, and inverted column bases. The title is on a panel that blocks off the central opening in a way typical of show architecture.

---

[1] *Wit's Recreations* (1640), epigrams 269, 270, in Sir John Suckling, *Works*, ed. Thomas Clayton (Oxford: Clarendon Press, 1971), i. 72. See Ian Donaldson, *Ben Jonson: A Life* (Oxford: Oxford University Press, 2011), 326–7. See Andrew Nash (ed.), *The Culture of Collected Editions* (London: Palgrave, 2003); William N. West, *Theatres and Encyclopedias in Early Modern Europe* (Cambridge: Cambridge University Press, 2003); Frances A. Yates, *Theatre of the World* (1969).

[2] See James Riddell, 'Ben Jonson's Folio of 1616', in Richard Harp and Stanley Stewart (eds), *The Cambridge Companion to Ben Jonson* (Cambridge: Cambridge University Press, 2000), 154.

[3] Stephen Orgel, 'Jonson and the Arts', in Harp and Stewart (eds), *The Cambridge Companion to Ben Jonson*, 144.

[4] See *OED*, s.v. *Pegma, pegme*: 'a kind of framework or stage used in theatrical displays or pageants, sometimes bearing an inscription'; John Florio, *Queen Anna's New World of Words* (1611; facsimile edn, Menston: Scolar, 1968), s.v. *Pegma*: 'a frame or pageant'.

Four Corinthian or composite columns rest on a high plinth recessed in the centre but with no stair by which entrance over the plinth might be effected. The columns—banded as in the so-called French order—have only the upper parts of the shafts fluted: the lower parts are carved, as in the uppermost columns of the Chateau of Anet's frontispiece.[5] The exotic form of column is not surprising in view of William Hole's unusual tastes: whereas most English engravers of his period were stylistically oriented to their Netherlandish contemporaries, Hole was 'more congenially allied to the French, and to the style of Leonard Gaultier in particular'.[6]

Inscriptions

The most conspicuous is the title itself. Beneath this, a motto is engraved in elegant italics: Hole was a celebrated lettering specialist, outstanding among the contemporary engravers who worked for writing-masters. He engraved the plates, for example, in Martin Billingsley's *The Pens Excellencie* (1618). Jonson's motto is proudly adapted from Horace, *Satires* 1.10.73–4: NEQUE, ME UT MIRETUR TURBA, LABORO: | CONTENTUS PAUCIS LECTORIBUS ('I do not strive to win the approval of the crowd, but am content with few readers').[7] Jonson profoundly identified with Horace, and translated the *Ars poetica*; his sobriquet 'the English Horace' was well earned.

The columns support an entablature broken in such a way that the frieze inscription is difficult to read. This perversely gives it a certain prominence: SINGULA QUAEQUE LOCUM TENEANT SORTITA DECENTER (Horace, *Ars poetica*, 92)—or, as Jonson translates it, 'each subject should retain | The place allotted to it, with decent praise'—words epitomizing the classical doctrine of decorum, or aptness.

---

[5] See Anthony Blunt, *Art and Architecture in France 1500 to 1700*, Pelican History of Art (London: Penguin, 1953; rev. edn, New Haven: Yale University Press, 1999), 30. For de l'Orme's and Vriedeman de Vries's versions of the French column, see Bernd Evers and Christof Thoenes (eds), *Architectural Theory from the Renaissance to the Present* (Cologne: Taschen, 2003), 218, 509.

[6] Arthur M. Hind, *Engraving in England in the Sixteenth and Seventeenth Centuries*, i. *The Tudor Period*; ii. *The Reign of James I*, 2 vols (1952–5), ii. 316–40.

[7] Horace's original is *neque te ut miretur turba labores | contentus paucis lectoribus.*

Medallions

There are two elaborately carved cartouches. In the upper cartouche, as Stephen Orgel observes, one might expect to find an author portrait. Instead, it shows a semi-cylindrical theatre. Herford and the Simpsons compare it to the Colosseum; but that was a four-storeyed amphitheatre and this has three tiers. A closer comparison is with the elegant Theatre of Marcellus completed by Augustus in 13 BC. Originally it had three storeys, although the uppermost tier and much of the rest disappeared in various rebuildings, including conversion to a *palazzo* in the sixteenth century. It was considered the most regular Roman building, and consequently used as a model for the orders.[8] Representations were available, for example, in Lafréry's *Speculum romanae magnificentiae*.[9] Other three-tier analogues include the Teatro Olympico at Vicenza and the Teatro Ducale at Sabionetta.

The lower cartouche, which occupies the space where the plinth breaks back in the centre, is inscribed with the imprint: LONDON: PRINTED BY WILLIAM STANSBY.[10]

Vignettes

The lower cartouche is flanked by two bas-reliefs on the plinth: vignettes labelled *plaustrum* and *visorium*. And, in the upper cartouche, a medallion frames a third vignette on the entablature, labelled *theatrum*. These vignettes appear to represent phases of the classical stage. *Plaustrum* ('wagon') alludes

---

[8] Roland Fréart de Chambray, *Parallèle de l'architecture antique et de la moderne* [...] (Paris, 1650), 13: by 'universal suffrage of those of the profession' the theatre of Marcellus was the most regular and conformable with Vitruvius'. See Vitruvius, 5.6.8; Evers and Thoenes (eds), *Architectural Theory*, 68, 75, 120.

[9] Antoine Lafréry (Antonio Lafreri), *Speculum romanae magnificentiae* (Rome: self-published, c.1575). For this highly mutable print album, see A. Grafton, G. W. Most, and S. Setti (eds), *The Classical Tradition* (Cambridge, MA: Belknap Press, 2010), 902–3.

[10] On the variants of the imprint ('Imprinte at London by Will Stansby'; 'London printed by W: Stansby, and are to be sould by Rich: Meighen'; 'London printed by William Stansby'), see Riddell, 'Ben Jonson's Folio of 1616', 159.

to the classic account of tragedy's origin, in Horace's *Ars poetica*.[11] As Jonson translates the passage:

> He too, that did in Treagicke Verse contend
> For the vile Goat, soone after forth did send
> The rough rude Satyrs naked, and would trye,
> Though sower, with safety of his gravity,
> How he could jest . . . (lines 311–15)

> Thespis is said to be the first found out
> The tragedy, and carried it about,
> Till then unknown, in carts, wherein did ride
> Those that did sing and act, their faces dyed
> With lees [dregs] of wine. (lines 391–5)

(Thespis, a sixth-century BC actor, was supposed to have introduced speaking parts.)

> Next Aeschilus, more late
> Brought in the visor, and the robe of state,
> Built a small-timber'd stage, and taught them talke
> Lofty, and great; and in the Buskin walk. (lines 395–8)

The term *tragodia* ('tragedy') was anciently thought to derive from Greek *tragos* ('he-goat'). Here, the L vignette shows a goat, perhaps won in the annual tragedy competition, trotting behind a pageant cart, pictured as a wagon of English design. A cask of wine, convenient for dying actors' faces, can be seen at the back of the wagon.

The R vignette shows a reconstruction of the earliest theatre, imagined as an elliptical amphitheatre excavated in the earth, with a central *orchestra* or dancing space for the chorus (here in modern dress). At the centre of the orchestra stands an altar to Dionysus with sacrificial fire. The chorus

---

[11] Lines 275–7: *Ignotum tragicae genus invenisse Camenae | dicitur et plaustris vexisse poemata Thespis, | quae canerent agerentque peruncti faecibus ora.*

consists of eight dancers, a number associated with Dionysus.[12] This amphitheatre's unhistorical shape reflects medieval and Renaissance fixation with circular forms. *Visorium* is not classical Latin,[13] and may be Jonson's coinage on the analogy of Greek *theasthai* ('spectate'), the root of *theatron* ('theatre'). More likely, however, Jonson took it from Ioannes Rosinus's *Antiquitatum Romanorum corpus*, as edited by Thomas Dempster, where *amphitheatrum* is glossed as *visorium*.[14] Drama's origin in a chorus of satyrs was vital for Jonson, since it sanctioned direct social satire, banned from Old Comedy.

Tableau

The main tableau consists of seven figures, five of them labelled. TRAGOE-DIA and COMOEDIA stand firmly on pedestals, occupying intercolumnar spaces in front of arches closed off by curtains (Tragedy's damasked, Comedy's plain). The haughty crowned figure representing Tragedy wears a robe over a knee-length tunic and a shorter tunic, both edged with lappets. Her conventionally high buskins have thick soles. She holds a sceptre, and her helmeted mask hangs on the outer column.

The comic Muse (partly modelled on Ripa's *Commedia*) also wears a lappeted tunic, over a full-length chiton or frock. With her R hand she holds a cloak that is slipping off her shoulder, and with her L leans on a rustic staff. On her feet are the traditional socks of comedy. Her elaborate coiffure is unusually intricate, and her mask is covered by a wide-brimmed hat. TRAGI-COMOEDIA aptly shares the clothes of Tragedy and Comedy—the crown

[12] Plutarch assigned the number eight to Dionysus since he was born in the eighth month; see Petrus Bungus, *Numerorum mysteria ex abditis plurimarum discipliarum fontibus hausta* [...] (Bergamo: Venturi, 1591), 324; Cornelius Agrippa, *De occulta philosophia libri tres*, ed. Vittoria Perrone Compagni (Leiden: Brill, 1992), 283, line 25: *hunc numerum Dionysio sacrum perhibent, qui octavo mense in lucem editus est.*

[13] Cf., however, *visor* ('viewer'), examples from AD 1194.

[14] Ioannes Rosinus, *Antiquitatum romanorum corpus* [1583], ed. Thomas Dempster (1613), 342, col. 2: *Amphitheatrum Latinis visorium quod commodissime ad ludicra convocatus, inde spectare posset.* Cassiodorus distinguished *amphitheatrum* from *theatrum*: *amphitheatrum rotundum est, theatrum vero ex medio amphitheatro est, semicirculi figuram habens.*

and sceptre, robe and lappeted tunic of the first, but the *chiton* and *socci* of the second.[15]

The emergent genre of tragicomedy had a more debatable place on Parnassus than either tragedy or comedy. It was scarcely recognized in ancient literary theory, although Euripides' tragedy *Alcestis* had a happy ending, and Plautus called his own *Amphytrion* a tragicomedy. In the Renaissance, however, Giraldi Cinthio (1504–73) praised the kind of tragedy ending in happiness as most suitable for performance. And Giovanni Battista Guarini (1538–1612) in his *Compendio della poesia tragicomica* (1601) argued for Tragicomedy as having better psychological effects on the passions. His own *Il Pastor Fido* (*c.*1585) had a great vogue in England, creating a fashion for plays with tragic main plots and comic subplots—the form Sidney dismissed as 'mongrel'. John Fletcher presents *The Faithful Shepherdess* (*c.*1609) as 'pastorall Tragie-comedie', explaining that 'a tragie-comedie is not so called in respect of mirth and kill-ing, but in respect it wants deaths, which is inough to make it no tragedie, yet brings some neere it, which is inough to make it no comedie'. But there were also hierarchical differences to be considered. In Jonson's title page Tragedy and Tragicomedy are crowned, to show they deal with royal or aristocratic characters, leaders of men.

Tragicomedy stands a little insecurely on the top edge of the upper car-touche, and so is closely juxtaposed with the Roman or modern theatre within the cartouche. Even more precariously supported are the figures flanking Tragicomedy, SATYR and PASTOR. The shepherd uses both hands to play his pan-pipe, while holding his crook between his legs and the car-touche. Satyrs like woodwouses were mythical creatures, half human and half bestial (half goat, according to Florio), who formed the sacred band of Dio-nysus and offered initiation into a community of this world and the next. The satyr's goatish side explains the impressively priapic staff between his legs.[16]

Satyrs formed the chorus of the ancient satyric drama, who were later imag-ined as impudent and outspoken—just as they show themselves in Jonson's *Oberon*.[17] There, in accordance with the Roman concept, they have 'cloven

---

[15] Allan H. Gilbert, *The Symbolic Persons in the Masques of Ben Jonson* (New York: AMS, 1969), 69, sees her as wearing one buskin and one *soccus*.

[16] Florio, *World of Words*, s.v. *satirione, satiriasmo*, which relates the satyr to *priapismo*.

[17] Ibid., s.v. *satira*: 'satire, an invective rebuking evils, and regarding no person', a feature important to Jonson the satiric dramatist.

feet, crooked legs, shaggy thighs, hairy tales, tawny wrists, stubbed horns, and pricking ears; in other words, they are conventional satyrs, as described by Casaubon'.[18] Later, John Dryden imagines the satyr as a 'rural god, made up betwixt a man and a goat; with a human head, hooked nose, pouting lips, a bunch or struma under the chin, pricked ears, and upright horns; the body shagged with hair, especially from the waist, and ending in a goat, with the legs and feet of that creature'.[19]

Satyric dramas such as Euripides' *Cyclops* were performed following a set of three tragedies. The satyrs were at once cruder and wiser than human beings: their father Silenus educated Dionysus. They were the first to sample Pan's pipes; and in Virgil's *Eclogue* 6 shepherds force from Silenus a song of poetry's power. So Jonson's pairing of satyr and shepherd suggests a musical contention between pastoral and satiric drama.

Pastoral drama, a creation of the Italian Renaissance, had a cast of satyrs as well as gods and shepherds and nymphs. Tasso's *Aminta* (1580) and Battista Guarini's *Il Pastor Fido* (1590) were immensely influential, and firmly established pastoral tragedy (Guarini called it tragicomedy) as a fashionable form. In England its exemplars include Fletcher's *The Faithful Shepherdess* (c.1609) and Jonson's *The Sad Shepherd* (1640, unfinished). Verse pastoral—as in Spenser's *The Shepheardes Calender* (1579)—was regarded as an allegorical and often satiric form using the speeches of 'homely persons' to 'insinuate and glance at greater matters [...] such as perchance had not been safe to have been disclosed in any other sort'.[20]

Jonson's shepherd and satyr, then, may both be satiric—*satiro* and *satira* were confused in the Renaissance.[21] And Orgel is partly right to see them as representing 'the third of the classic genres, the satiric or pastoral'.[22] But satyrs and shepherds were also distinct, as different as sheep and goats in the

[18] Gilbert, *Symbolic Persons*, 212. Jonson owned a copy of Casaubon's notes on Athenaeus, and studied them for *Oberon*; see ibid. 216, and David McPherson, 'Ben Jonson's Library and Marginalia', *Studies in Philology*, 71 (1974), 33 (item 34).

[19] John Dryden, *A Discourse Concerning Satyre*, ed. George Watson (Dent, 1962), ii. 97–8.

[20] George Puttenham, *The Art of English Poesy*, ed. Frank Whigham and Wayne A. Rebhorn (Ithaca, NY: Cornell University Press, 2007), bk 1, ch. 18, p. 128.

[21] See *OED* s.v. *Satyr*, 1. c. They are distinguished however in Florio, *World of Words*, s.v. *satira*, *satiro*, and *satire*.

[22] Orgel, 'Jonson and the Arts', 144.

biblical parable. A common association of the satyr is captured by Edward Guilpin's phrase 'Satyre-footed gull' (*Skialetheia*, Satyre 1). Guilpin encourages his Muse to quicken her pace: 'Thys leaden-heeled passion is to[o] dull, | To keepe pace with this Satyre-footed gull'. *Gull* seems already to mean 'con-man, trickster'. His satyr is reprehensible, in contrast with the pastoral ideals of *Il Pastor Fido* or *The Faithful Shepherdess* with its fine shades of chastity.[23]

Herford and the Simpsons assume that Jonson's title page presents personifications of the different kinds of drama exemplified in the ensuing book. But this makes the prominence of Tragicomedy problematic, for Jonson never wrote a tragicomedy. More likely the title page, like many of its time, is encyclopaedic. It represents literature and drama in all their variety, and so refers as much to Jonson's poems as to his plays and masques. Pastoral can be found in 'To Penshurst', and satire in many of the *Epigrams*. The theatre itself, indeed, was often thought of in a general way as a gathering of previous knowledge and a site where new contributions might be displayed.[24]

To Elizabethans, tragicomedy was an elite taste. Fletcher's *The Faithful Shepherdess* was poorly received—in Jonson's view, because it did not satisfy the popular expectation of sexual titillation. Yet he praised it in a commendatory poem, and regarded it as 'a tragicomedy well done'.[25] For the sophisticated, tragicomedy was the cutting edge of drama. The *Compendio della poesia tragicomica* of Battista Guarini (1538–1612) validated it as a new form, exempt from Aristotle's rules and more suited to the modern age.[26] Jonson too may have recognized it as an emergent form: 'I see not then but we should enjoy the same *licentia*, or free power, to illustrate and heighten our invention as they [the ancients] did; and not be tied to those strict and regular forms which the niceness of a few (who are nothing but form) would thrust upon us.'[27] Here, as often, Jonson shows his awareness of genre as changing:

[23] Cf. Isa. 13: 21; Shakespeare, *Hamlet* 1. 2. 140.

[24] Cf. Donaldson, *Ben Jonson*, 327–9; Frances A. Yates, *Theatre of the World* (London: Routledge & Kegan Paul, 1969); Ann Blair, *The Theater of Nature: Jean Bodin and Renaissance Science* (Princeton: Princeton University Press, 1997).

[25] *The Cambridge Edition of the Works of Ben Jonson*, ed. David Bevington et al., 7 vols (Cambridge: Cambridge University Press, 2012), iii. 372; v. 371, lines 170–1.

[26] Gilbert, *Symbolic Persons*, 236.

[27] *Every Man out of his Humour*, Induction, in *Works*, i. 272.

a form with a long and continuing history. Everywhere in his multifarious title page ancient and modern images mingle.

Flanking Tragicomedy are two tiny figures in the niches of the highest structure: on the L, Dionysus or Bacchus, recognizable from his thyrsus and ivy leaves; on the R, Apollo, with light rays round his head. (Perhaps it was prudent not to make them more noticeable, since they were after all pagan idols.) Anciently, Dionysus presided over dramatic performances. Apollo, as leader of the Muses, holds a *bassa lira* or *lira da braccio* and bow or plectrum, as in Raphael's *Parnassus* fresco.[28] The lyre might indicate a patron of Poesia; but Apollo often appears with it in contests with Pan.[29]

Printer

William Stansby was a printer and bookseller in London from 1597 until his death in 1638. At first apprenticed to John Windet, he acquired a share of the business by 1609, and succeeded to it in the following year. Stansby's establishment was one of the largest presses in London, famous for its specialist team of compositors in Anglo-Saxon, Greek, and Hebrew, as well as Japanese. The high quality of Stansby's printing made him an obvious choice for Jonson's ambitious *Workes*—and for its frontispiece with its fine detail.

Stansby printed other celebrated poetical and historical books, by John Donne, Michael Drayton, William Camden, Sir Walter Ralegh, and Sir Francis Bacon. In the year when he published Jonson's 1616 *Workes*, he printed nearly thirty books; he had not yet incurred the wrath of the authorities by printing John Selden's *History of Tithes*. He worked at Paul's Wharf at the Cross Keys, and lived in Thames Street, next to St Peter's church. This was at the opposite end of Paul's Chain from St Paul's Churchyard, where many booksellers had their places of business.[30]

---

[28] See Emanuel Winternitz, *Musical Instruments and their Symbolism in Western Art* (London: Faber, 1967), 89–90 and pl. 84.

[29] Orgel sees the two deities as patrons of ecstatic and rational theatre.

[30] Richard Bishop acquired the establishment in 1636, and printed the second edition of Jonson's Works.

Designer

Who designed the 1616 title page? The engraver William Hole (d. 1624), Chief Engraver of the Mint and Graver of the King's seals, was a man of culture, enjoying terms of friendship with many writers and musicians of his time. He had engraved the title page and some of the maps for the 1607 edition of William Camden's *Britannia*. And he doubtless made many contributions to Jonson's 1616 title page—in matters of costume and architecture, for example. The rather wooden figures are characteristic of his work. But he can hardly have designed the entire title page. Only Jonson himself had the learning and the perspective on theatre history for that. Whether Jonson coined the term *visorium* or borrowed it, his responsibility for the overall design seems certain.

FRANCISCI
DE VERULAMIO,
Summi Angliæ
CANCELLARIJ,
Instauratio
magna.

Multi pertransibunt & augebitur scientia.

Sim. Pass. sculp.

Anno

LONDINI
Apud Joannem Billium
Typographum
Regium.

1620

Francis Bacon
INSTAURATIO MAGNA
1620

The reputation of Francis Bacon (1561–1626) as a philosopher of science has fluctuated greatly. In the seventeenth century he was the Moses of the Royal Society to Thomas Spratt, and a powerful influence on continental scientists such as Constantijn Huygens (1596–1657). His doctrine of non-speculative method authorized Isaac Newton (1642–1727) to avoid accumulation of hypotheses. In the eighteenth century he provided a classification of knowledge to the French encyclopaedists. But in the nineteenth century he was severely criticized for pursuing knowledge of natural philosophy; and modern critics have attacked his emphasis on accumulation of facts. However understandable this critique may be, it does less than justice to the rich variety of Bacon's vision of science, or to the originality of his counter-speculative method—his 'bringing things down to practice'.[1] The *Instauratio magna* (1620) gives an overview of his immense scheme of reforming science, parts of which are further developed in his other works.

Tableau

The title page of *Instauratio magna* ('the great renewal') shows two Tuscan or Doric columns rising from square bases standing on opposite strips of land with a channel between leading to open sea, in which sea monsters and a spouting whale disport themselves. In Simon de Passe's superb engraving, a ship with sails set and flying the four-banded English ensign returns from the open sea, and another can be seen near the horizon. Approaching the channel is a ship that has been described as sailing forth.[2] However, the ship, an armed merchantman, is clearly returning from a voyage. It is a three-masted galleon with a high aftercastle, but without the earlier carrack's high forecastle.[3] Another similar ship is near the horizon, thus illustrating the 'thorough passage' over the ocean referred to in an inscription.

Bacon's *Sylva sylvarum* (1627) has quite a similar title plate. Its engraver was Thomas Cecill (worked 1626–40), who probably copied it from Simon de Passe. *Sylva* was published posthumously, by Dr William Rawley (*c.*1588–1667), Bacon's chaplain and editor. Rawley worked through the bookseller and stationer William Lee 2nd, of Great Turk's Head near the Mitre tavern.

In *Sylva*, the pillars stand on square plinths with ovals on each face, unlike the squares of the *Instauratio* plinths. They are much more ornate—Corinthian columns, with a band dividing each shaft in octave proportion. The upper portions are fluted, the lower decorated with acanthus, medallions, and ogival mouldings. Between the pillars is a sphere inscribed MUNDUS INTELLEC-TUALIS, and a cartouche framing the title. The sphere is illuminated by the

---

[1] Francis Bacon, *The* Instauratio magna, *Part II:* Novum Organum *and Associated Texts*, ed. Graham Rees with Maria Wakely. *The Oxford Francis Bacon*, xi (Oxford: Clarendon Press, 2004), 94.

[2] Sir Peter Medawar, 'The Effecting of all Things Possible', *Listener* (2 Oct. 1969); Corbett and Lightbown, 186.

[3] Irene de Groot and Robert Vorstman, *Maritime Prints by the Dutch Masters* (London: Gordon Fraser, 1980), fig. 4a and glossary.

divine source of light, the Tetragrammaton or name of God, between two cherubim, 'the angels of knowledge and illumination'.[4] The whole tableau is more pious and explicitly religious than that of the *Instauratio*: it had to counter the opposition to natural philosophy. Rawlay used a similar title page because he believed the *Sylva sylvarum* or natural history was intended by Bacon to form a part of the *Instauratio Magna*: 'This *Naturall History* was [...] Designed and set down for a third part of the *Instauration*'.[5]

Behind these resemblances lies a common source: the famous *impresa* of Charles V, with its two pillars and the motto *plus oultre*. This refers to the pillars of Hercules, who in the course of his tenth labour set them up to show other travellers how far he had been. *Ne plus ultra* ('nothing beyond') set a limit to the ancient world. The allusive motto expressed the idea of going beyond the limit of the known world; thus referring to the discovery of America and the establishment of the Hispanic empire in the new world. (The image of two columns appeared on the Spanish dollar, and survives to this day on the US dollar bill.) Charles adopted the motto *plus oultre* on the advice of Luigi Marliano his doctor, perhaps to encourage risk-taking. The *impresa* appeared everywhere—in the panelling of the Alhambra palace, even in the arms of Spain.[6]

Charles's *impresa* was known in England from Claude Paradin's *Devises heroïques*, translated into English by P.S., from a Latin version.[7] Paradin's *pictura* is a pair of fluted composite columns standing on a perfunctory strip of land. As he explains, Hercules forced a passage through the mountain range separating the Mediterranean and the Atlantic. Columns of bronze were to mark the limit of the world. According to Paradin, the emperor's motto implied his hope of further conquests beyond (*plus oultre*).

Bacon always connected the pillars of Hercules, 'the figurative denial of their prohibition (*non ultra*), and the Daniel prophecy'.[8] He applied the

---

[4] *The Advancement of Learning* (1605), i. 27, cit. Corbett and Lightbown, 185–6.

[5] Francis Bacon, *Sylva sylvarum: Or a Natural Historie. In Ten Centuries* (London: W. Rawley, 1627), sig. A^v.

[6] See Earl Rosenthal, *The Palace of Charles V in Granada* (Princeton: Princeton University Press, 1985).

[7] Claude Paradin, *Devises heroïques* (Lyons, 1557), 29–31; ed. Alison Saunders (Menston: Scolar, 1989).

[8] Bacon, *Instauratio magna*, 489, 492.

impresa metaphorically: his title plate refers to increase of knowledge, not geographical expansion. The strips of land are strewn with pebbles and shells; the returning merchantman doubtless brings a freight of new information.

Inscriptions

The book's title is inscribed on the sky itself, between the two columns: FRANCISCI DE VERULAMIO SUMMI ANGLIAE CANCELLARII INSTAURATIO MAGNA ('The great instauration of Francis of St Albans, Lord Chancellor of England'). Bacon had become Lord Chancellor in January 1618.

In a cartouche at the very foot of the engraving is the epigraph MULTI PERTRANSIBUNT ET AUGEBITUR SCIENTIA (Daniel 12: 4: 'Many shall run to and fro, and knowledge shall be increased'). When Daniel enquires as to the meaning of the prophecy, he is told the words are sealed until the time of the end. To the L of the cartouche is inscribed SIM [ON DE] PASSE SCULPT [IT] ('engraved it').

Below the engraving is a frame with another cartouche, flanked by two framed inscriptions, ANNO and 1620. This lower cartouche, decorated with rosettes, pearls, and shells, bears the inscription LONDINI APUD JOANNEM BILLIUM, TYPOGRAPHER REGIUM.

Engraver

The engraver was Simon de Passe (1595–1647), son of Crispijn de Passe (1564–1637) and Magdalene de Bock. Crispijn was a prominent Cologne engraver until exiled because of his anabaptism. Simon worked in London (1616–22) and became a fine portraitist. Among the subjects of his fifty-seven portraits are Queen Anne on horseback, the duke of Buckingham, and Francis Bacon. He left London to work in Utrecht, and left Utrecht to be royal engraver to Christian IV of Denmark.[9]

---

[9] See Ilja M. Veldman, in *ODNB*; A. M. Hind, *Engraving in England in the Sixteenth and Seventeenth Centuries*, 2 vols (Cambridge: Cambridge University Press, 1952–5), ii. 245–301; D. Franken, *L'Œuvre gravé de van de Passe* (Amsterdam, 1881).

Printer

John Bill 1, bookseller and printer 1604–30 in London, was the printer. From 1616 Bill was one of the king's Printers. He worked in St Paul's Churchyard in 1605 with John Norton previously his master. As a King's Printer, Bill was allowed to own four presses. Although using these to the full entailed a complicated printing schedule, it saved time and made it possible to give the care and attention that combining letterpress with engraving called for—as the high quality of the frontispiece shows.

Tempora cinxiss et Foliorum densior umbra,
Debeter Genio Laurea Sylva tuo.
Tempora et Illa Tibi mollis redimisset Oliva,
Scilicet excludis Versibus Arma tuis.
Admisces Antiqua Novis, Iucunda Severis,
Hinc Iuvenis discat, Fœmina Virgo Senex.
Ut solo minor es Phœbo, si major es Unus
Omnibus, Ingenio Mente, Lepore, Stylo.
scripsit I.H.C. W.M.

Robert Herrick

Robert Herrick
HESPERIDES
1648

The frontispiece to *Hesperides* adopted a design popularized by the book-seller Humphrey Moseley, who was from 1645 the outstanding literary publisher. This design, featuring an author portrait, was followed by the engraver William Marshall in editions of many eminent poets and dramatists of the period, including Milton, Crashaw, Suckling, Beaumont and Fletcher, Middleton, Cowley, and Denham.

The *Hesperides* frontispiece bears a particular resemblance to that of Thomas Stephens's *Essay on Statius*, also engraved by Marshall and published in 1648.[1] In both, the poet being honoured with laurel wreaths is represented as a bust on a monumental plinth. In the case of Statius, the poet is already

---

[1] Reproduced in *The Grolier Club's Catalogue of Original and Early Editions of Some of the Poetical and Prose Works of English Writers from Langland to Prior*, 4 vols in 1 (London: Holland Press, 1964), iii. 130.

crowned: the additional wreath Minerva brings may be intended for the trans-lator, Stephens. In the *Hesperides* frontispiece Herrick eyes a wreath offered by a flying putto, while behind him another putto holds another wreath. Herrick being a love poet, *amorini* may have seemed more appropriate than Minerva.

The hook-nosed, curly-headed, and moustached figure has too many dis-tinguishing features to be a 'generalized representation of a poet', as J. Max Patrick suggests.[2] Besides, Moseley encouraged an expectation that author portraits should be based on good likenesses.[3] But Herrick may have wished to present himself half seriously as an avatar of Ovidius *Naso*.[4] Ruth Connolly and Thomas Cain observe that, 'unlike most of Moseley's output, Herrick's image is not reproduced as the portrait of a living poet but as a bust in a Parnassian garden'.[5] Any idea of Herrick as a 'modern classic' would of course be anachronistic. In any case, several of Marshall's frontispieces present the author's portrait as a bust—for example, Thomas Randolph's *Poems* (1638, 1640), Michael Drayton's *Poems* (1637), and Stephens's *Essay*.[6]

Emblems

The frontispiece portrays a landscape with many poetic associations. In post-classical art, Helicon and Parnassus were commonly conflated.[7] Here, the designer has combined Helicon with Parnassus, Hippocrene with the Castalian fount. Norman Farmer thinks 'that the hill must be Helicon and that the

---

[2] Robert Herrick, *The Complete Poetry*, ed. J. Max Patrick (1963; New York: Norton, 1968), 7.

[3] Norman Farmer compares Marshall's likeness of Suckling: see his 'Herrick's Hesperidean Garden: *ut pictura poesis* Applied', in R. B. Rollin and J. Max Patrick (eds), *'Trust to Good Verses': Herrick Tercentenary Essays* (Pittsburgh: University of Pittsburgh Press, 1978), 28.

[4] Cf. Robert Herrick, *The Complete Poetry*, ed. Tom Cain and Ruth Connolly (Oxford: Clarendon Press, 2013), i, p. lxx, poem 201, line 24. Stephen Dobranski, *Readers and Authorship in Early Modern England* (Cambridge: Cambridge University Press, 2005), 161–3, and Syrithe Pugh, 'Ovidian Exile in the *Hesperides*: Herrick's Politics of Intertextuality', *Review of English Studies*, 57 (2006), 736, assume the pun on Publius Ovidius *Naso*.

[5] Ruth Connolly and Tom Cain (eds), *'Lords of Wine and Oile': Community and Conviviality in the Poetry of Robert Herrick* (Oxford: Oxford University Press, 2011), 17.

[6] Marshall, in Johnson, *Catalogue*, nos III, 78, 39.   [7] See *OGCM* ii. 847.

spring flowing from its base is Hippocrene, the waters of which are released by the hard hoof of Pegasus and are sacred to the nine Muses'.[8] But this Pegasus, although taking off in an excited state, strikes no stream from the hilltop. Instead, the stream issues from a cave at the foot of the hill. Max Patrick writes of 'naked figures—presumably the Muses'.[9] The Muses more usually danced in a group of nine, as in Mantegna's *Parnassus*; but four or five Muses dancing can be paralleled. The cave in the frontispiece is the Corycian Antrum on Mount Parnassus, sacred to Pan and the nymphs; the stream is the Castalian spring of poetic inspiration. In fact, the landscape represents no single place in classical mythology.

Several familiar emblems of inspiration are drawn on, such as Dionysius Lebey-Batilly's *Emblemata* (1596), emblem 49, showing Pegasus rising from Mount Helicon. The grouping of Hippocrene and Castalia may have come from such syncretistic sources as Juan de Horozco's *Emblemas morales* (Segovia, 1591): 'the spirit of poetry may be imbibed from the river of many names in that country: "Castalia after the Muses, to whom it was consecrated, Heliconia after the place where it was situated, Pegasia and Hippocrene after the myths about the horse Pegasus"'.[10]

The garden of the Hesperides was a natural metaphor for literary anthologies: Humphrey Moseley commissioned one such, a literary commonplace book called *Hesperides, or the Muses Garden*.[11] But Herrick was inspired by dead poets in a more personal way. In 'Supping with Ghosts' Syrithe Pugh discusses his aspiration to imitate ancient poets so intimately as to join them in a poetic Elysium.[12] Indeed, his title alludes to a Hesperidean garden often identified with Elysium itself.[13]

Herrick reaches out to this Elysium of congenial poets. He explores the transmigration of ancient souls—especially Anacreon's and Ovid's—through imitation and identification, 'convivial [...] exchanges between living and dead

---

[8] Rollin and Max Patrick (eds), *'Trust to Good Verses'*, 31.

[9] Herrick, *Complete Poetry*, ed. Cain and Connolly, 7.

[10] See Robert Clements, *Picta Poesis*, Temi e Testi, 6 (Rome: Edizioni di storia e letteratura, 1960), 55. The symbolism was familiar enough from Ovid, *Metamorphoses* (5.254–64) as to appear on medals such as Bembo's (Hill 484b).

[11] Connolly and Cain (eds), *'Lords of Wine and Oile'*, 16.

[12] Syrithe Pugh, 'Supping with Ghosts', in ibid. 222.   [13] Ibid. 16.

poets'.[14] In 'The Apparition of his Mistress' Herrick imagines Anacreon intoxicated to the point of impotence ('cup-shot'), until he angers the 'young enchantress' or Muse: snatching Anacreon's crown, she 'gave the wreath to me'. Herrick seems to think he may do better through his more tempered 'cleanly wantonness'. A comparable reaching-out to the dead appears in his Charon dialogues and in his 'greeny calendar' of dead friends. But, if the frontispiece bust were to raise any idea of Herrick as already among the dead, it would be dispelled by the playfulness of his portrait.

Inscriptions

The plinth supporting the poet's bust and flanked by two *amorini* with laurel branches is inscribed with Latin verses by John Harmar (*c.*1594–1670), an anti-Laudian intruded as Professor of Greek at Oxford in 1650. On graduating MA, Harmar took orders and became an usher at Magdalen College School. Later he was appointed master of St Alban's Free School (1626) and under-master of Westminster School (1632). He wrote grammatical texts, and a Greek *Lexicon* (1637). Wood calls him an excellent philologist, happy in translating from Greek and Latin, and says he translated plays by Margaret Cavendish, duchess of Newcastle.[15] Herrick addressed Harmar in an epigram 'To His learned friend [...]' (H966).

1. The translation of Harmar's inscription by Cain and Connolly, much superior to Grosart's, brings out the adverse circumstances:

> A denser shade of leaves should have bound your temples:
> Your Genius deserves a Laurel Grove.
> The peaceful olive should have encircled those brows of yours:
> For certainly war is banished from your verses.
> You mix the old with the new, the playful with the serious:
> Hence the young man, the woman, the virgin, the old man may learn

---

[14] Stella Achilleos, ' "Ile bring thee *Herrick* to *Anacreon*": Robert Herrick's Anacreontics and the Politics of Conviviality', in Connolly and Cain (eds), '*Lords of Wine and Oile*', 193.

[15] See Elisabeth Leedham-Green, in *ODNB*.

That as you are only less than Phoebus, so you stand out greater
Than all the rest in genius, intellect, wit and style.[16]

The subjunctives stress what should have happened in better times: the recognition of laurels would have been more ample—a whole grove.

2. On the title page itself, the first inscription is HESPERIDES, a name with many associations. The three Hesperides, daughters of Hesperus, were guardians of the golden apples Juno gave to Jupiter on their wedding day. Their garden far in the west is geographically appropriate to Herrick's Dean Prior in Devon. And it had Royalist associations with the western *insulae fortunatae*, an Elysium identified with the Britain of James I, 'fair Beauty's gardens' and 'Loves Hesperides'.[17] Jonson had identified Hesperus as the evening star with James; Herrick extended this to Charles I: on the Prince's natal day Venus was visible all day long—the 'silver Star' seen at 'Noon of Day'.[18]

In the Hesperidean garden grew the apples of virgin beauty to be reached only by Hercules: an allegory familiar from mythological texts such as Ovid's *Metamorphoses* (5. 254–64) and from emblems such as Alciati's *Custodiendas virgines*:

This is the true likeness of unwedded Pallas. Hers is this dragon, standing at its mistress's feet. Why is this animal the goddess's companion? Its allotted task is to guard things. Thus it cares for groves and sacred temples. Sleepless care is needed to keep girls safe before marriage; love spreads his snares everywhere.[19]

As C. S. Lewis remarks of the dragon, 'the Hesperides themselves associate it with virginity'.[20] And Claude Mignault's commentary on Alciati adds that

---

[16] Herrick, *Complete Poetry*, ed. Cain and Connolly, i, p. lxxi.

[17] Thomas Carew, *Coelum Britannicum* (London, 1634), line 946 *et passim*.

[18] Herrick, *Complete Poetry*, ed. Cain and Connolly, poem 213, line 20.

[19] Andrea Alciati, *Emblematum liber* (Augsburg: Steyner, 1531), emblem 43; *Emblemata cum commentariis* (Padua: Pietro Paolo Tozzi,, 1621; repr. New York and London: Garland, 1976), emblem 22.

[20] C. S. Lewis, *Studies in Medieval and Renaissance Literature*, ed. Walter Hooper (Cambridge: Cambridge University Press, 1966), 166.

'the apples of the Hesperides were guarded by the dragon night and day' (*a dracone pervigili custodiebantur*)'.[21] In a word, *Hesperides* was the aptest of titles for love poems characterized by 'cleanly wantonness'.

3. The subtitle, THE WORKS BOTH HUMANE & DIVINE OF ROBERT HERRICK ESQ., is remarkable in that this is one of the first volumes of poetry to be called Works.

4. The epigraph modifies the usual early modern reading of an Ovidian verse (*Amores* 3.9.28), *defugiunt avidos carmina sola rogos* ('Only songs escape the greedy funeral pyres'). Herrick's altered version, EFFUGIENT AVIDOS CARMINA NOSTRA ROGOS ('Our songs will escape the greedy funeral pyres'), is more confident.[22]

Stationers

Herrick's publishers were John Williams (fl. 1635–78) and Francis Eglesfield (1637–88), who may have acquired Andrew Crooke's rights to Herrick's poems. Both were apprenticed to James and Anne Boler. Williams was freed 1627, and worked at the Crane in St Paul's Churchyard from 1636. Eglesfield was freed later, and worked at the Marigold in Goldsmith's Row in Cheapside and in St Paul's Churchyard. Part of the *Hesperides* edition was sold by Thomas Hunt, an Exeter bookseller who was able to exploit Herrick's local reputation in Royalist Devon. Like a fifth of books published in the period, *Hesperides* was never entered in the Stationers' Register—unless it was the same as *Several Poems*, entered 29 April 1640. A special reason for not entering *Hesperides* may have been the Royalist commitments of its stationers, engraver, and printer: they would have been wary of offering the book to the licensers.

The leading investor was probably John Williams, He was known to Herrick through their common acquaintance Thomas Fuller, and through his father, William Williams (a leading Cambridge stationer during Herrick's time as a student). Although *Hesperides* includes only a few political poems, the

[21] Alciati, *Emblemata cum commentariis*, 597, emblem 138.
[22] For previous uses of this Ovidian verse as an epigraph, by Drayton (twice), Du Bartas, and William Gager, see Herrrick, *Complete Poetry*, ed. Cain and Connolly, i, p. lxxv.

publication was ideologically significant through Herrick's being a prominent poet and an Anglican displaced from his benefice.

John Williams's sign, the Crown, appears on the title page.[23] But the Large
Crown used for the *Hesperides* title page was more special: it probably should
be seen as an expression of loyalty. Newly cut, it is the St Edward's crown
Charles I had been crowned with in 1625: the same crown that appears fallen
to the ground in the frontispiece of *Eikon basilike*. After 1650 Williams seldom used the Large Crown woodblock; but in 1660 he used it again for
Thomas Fuller's *A Happy Handful*.

Printer

Herrick's printer has recently been identified by Cain and Connolly as John
Grismond, on the basis of his using certain sorts of type and ornaments.
Flower ornaments could have been borrowed; but a distinctive *W*, also used
in *Eikon basilike*, is decisive. Grismond was freed from apprenticeship to
Miles Flesher or Fletcher in 1641; his printing house was the Angel, north of
St Paul's Churchyard. He worked for the Royalist stationer Richard Royston,
and was frequently in trouble with the Council of State for printing pro-
Royalist pamphlets.[24]

Engraver

Herrick's engraver was William Marshall (fl. 1617–49), who worked on commission for the London book trade, engraving frontispieces for many first
editions of famous authors. Yet his work was of a low quality, except when
he could copy from a good model: he was seldom commissioned by print
publishers. His style resembles that of Netherlandish incomers such as Simon
de Passe or Francis Delaram; but he was not a great draughtsman. Whether
because of incompetence or political prejudice, Marshall engraved an unpleas-
ant portrait of John Milton for the *Poems, English and Latin* (1645). Milton,

---

[23] See Herrick, *Complete Poetry*, ed. Cain and Connolly, i. 405–6.
[24] Ibid. i. 406–11.

who was vain about his appearance, responded with a cruel practical joke. He wrote a Greek epigram describing the portrait as 'the poor portrayal of a poor engraver', and arranged for Marshall, who was innocent of Greek, to engrave it below the portrait. Not content with this revenge, Milton later criticized Marshall's portrait of Charles in *Eikon basilike* for its 'quaint emblems'.

Nevertheless, the prolific Marshall is credited with more than 250 plates, mostly title pages or portrait frontispieces.[25] He worked on editions of many of the foremost literary figures, including Peter Heylin, James I, Philemon Holland, John Donne, Michael Drayton, Sir Thomas More, Thomas Fuller, Francis Bacon, George Herbert, Ben Jonson, Sir Thomas Browne, Jeremy Taylor, and Mildmay Fane. As many as eight of Marshall's frontispieces, strikingly, were to books of emblems.[26] His most famous work was the frontispiece to *Eikon basilike* (1645), purporting to be written by Charles I: it was reprinted fifty-seven times.

Designers

Cain and Connolly assume that 'the iconography is almost certainly Herrick's'. But Herrick had nothing to do with the closely similar frontispiece to Thomas Stephens's *Essay on Statius*, engraved by Marshall in the same year as *Hesperides*. Clearly the engraver contributed to the designing of the *Hesperides* frontispiece. After all, Herrick had no experience of publication, whereas Marshall, for all his limitations, was one of the most experienced engravers in the London book trade, and had a special interest in emblems. The conclusion seems inescapable that Marshall and Herrick, together with John Williams, collaborated in designing the *Hesperides* frontispiece.

[25] See Antony Griffiths, in *ODNB*. Johnson, *Catalogue*, lists 114 frontispieces by Marshall, from 1617 to 1649.

[26] In Johnson, *Catalogue*: Quarles (nos 25, 57, 98, 99, 110); Wither (no. 29); Estienne (no. 96); Fane (no. 107).

Thomas Hobbes
LEVIATHAN
1651

*L*eviathan is among the greatest works of political philosophy in our literature, and perhaps the most original. The book had its occasion from
a debate between exiled Royalists as to what powers (if any) Charles should
concede to reach accord with the Commonwealth. Hobbes's view was that
power over the army should not be surrendered: 'command of the Militia,
without other Institution, maketh him that hath it Soveraign.'[1] And he held
that 'the monarch must control the Church, because the people are "governed
by the pulpit"'. In particular, to accept a Presbyterian system would give away
the power of the pulpit. Thus, on most points Hobbes agreed with the king's
position.

This is reflected in the ten symbols in the compartments of the title page.
Hobbes's views were inherently Royalist; although he cautiously defined

---

[1] Thomas Hobbes, *Leviathan*, ed. Noel Malcolm, 3 vols (Oxford: Clarendon Press, 2012), i. 92.

'sovereign' to mean that of a single person or an assembly, monarchy, or republicanism. Similar caution may explain the darkness of some of the symbolism in the compartments.

This is one of the best-known title pages in English literature; yet many of its features remain unexplained. The upper register represents the political Leviathan dominating a symbolic landscape. He holds both a sword and a crozier. The lower register is divided into ten compartments with vignettes and emblems, secular and ecclesiastical.

The compartmented frontispiece may have originated from Germany, but was familiar in England through the Bishops' Bible (1568), and more widely popular from the 1620s. The compartments advertised topics of the book to follow, dividing them into categories. A well-known example is Robert Burton's *Anatomy of Melancholy* (1628), where this function is spelt out in a prefatory 'argument', or explanation.

Hobbes's title-page compartments number ten, arranged in two columns of five each. The arrangement by decade was standard, and implied its use as an aide-memoire. In Jonson's *The Case is Altered*, Francisco says: 'I will be silent, yet that I may serve | But as a Decade in the art of memory.'[2] Here, the topics of the L column, positioned under Leviathan's sword, address aspects of temporal power: castle; crown; cannon; a trophy of military equipment and symbols (flags, muskets, pikes, swords, drums, fasces); and battle, the final recourse of power, or of challenge to it. Thus, circular forms, expressive of unity, are evident in all the L compartments except the last.[3]

The R column, concerned with church governance, is harder to interpret. The compartments show 1. a church; 2. a bishop's mitre; 3. the thunderbolt of excommunication, the ultimate exercise of episcopal authority; 4. tools of dialectic; 5. a contemporary disputation between clerics (conflict corresponding to battle in the temporal sphere). There are two pairs of disputants; one figure, arguing from authority, holds a book. The doctors wear bonnets and gowns.[4]

The fourth compartment on the R calls for further comment. The trident and variously shaped forks indicate the divisions and dichotomies of logical debate. All are inscribed: the trident with SYL-LOGIS-ME; the straight

---

[2] Herford and Simpson, ix. 315–16; cf. Introduction: Compartments.
[3] Hobbes, *Leviathan*, ed. Malcolm, i. 130.   [4] Corbett and Lightbown, 221.

central fork with SPIRITUAL and TEMPORAL; the R, straight-tined fork with REAL and INTENTIONAL; and the asymmetric fork with DIRECT and INDIRECT. Beneath are literal, animal horns inscribed DI-LEM-MA.

So much is evident. But the compartments have more to show, for the objects in the fourth are all from the visual alphabets of Johannes Host von Romberch, a fifteenth-century Dominican (Fig. 14). These alphabets were used to form words to be memorized. In one example, illustrated by Frances Yates, '*Conti* (*nentia*) is remembered by the inscription on her chest in the "objects" alphabet'.[5] In *Leviathan*, the forks spell NVMN, suggesting NVM(I) N(IS), Latin for 'divine power or majesty' (*OLD* 4). Thus the fourth compartment encapsulates the theme of *Leviathan*: that the power of the state protects the subjects, who surrender their individual will to its sovereign authority.

Inscriptions

The engraved title page contains three inscriptions. At the upper edge is a biblical quotation: NON EST POTESTAS SUPER TERRAM QUAE COMPARETUR EI IOB 41. 24 ('There is no power on earth that may be compared to it'). The biblical text is from the Vulgate version with one slight variation of word order: POTESTAS SUPER TERRAM instead of SUPER TERRAM POTESTAS. Hobbes uses Leviathan as an allegory of the state, and may have thought this the sense of the biblical passage.[6]

A second inscription fills the richly ornamented fringed cloth suspended from the central portion of the compartmented frame occupying the page's lower half. It reads LEVIATHAN OR THE MATTER, FORME AND POWER OF A COMMONWEALTH ECCLESIASTICALL AND CIVIL. BY THOMAS HOBBES OF MALMESBURY. The third inscription, on a cartouche filling the space below the cloth, gives the imprint: LONDON PRINTED FOR ANDREW CROOKE 1651. The manuscript version of the title page omits the biblical epigraph and gives the inscription in the cartouche as ANNO CHRISTI 1651.

---

[5] Frances A. Yates, *The Art of Memory* (London: Routledge & Kegan Paul, 1966), 120, figs 6 a, b, c; Mary J. Carruthers, *The Book of Memory: A Study of Memory in Medieval Culture* (Cambridge: Cambridge University Press, 1990), 127.

[6] See Hobbes, *Leviathan*, ed. Malcolm, i. 114–15; Corbett and Lightbown, 223–4.

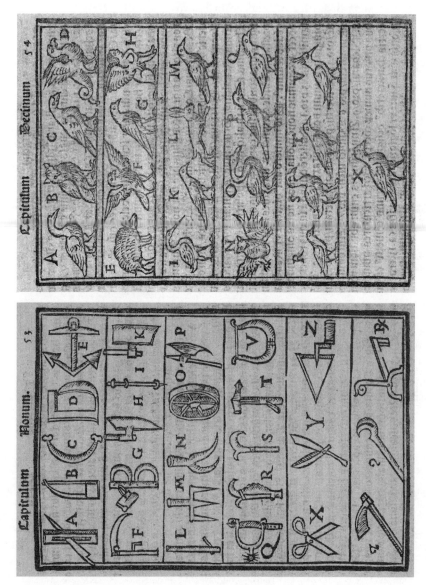

Fig. 14. Memory alphabet, Romberch, *Congestorium* (Venice, 1533), 120. Courtesy of the Bodleian Libraries, The University of Oxford.

Publication

Leviathan was licensed in January 1651 by John Downham, theologian and licenser of books of divinity. Downham was a lax licenser, who probably read little of the book. Its copyright was allowed by Philemon Stephens, Warden of the Stationers' Company. Hobbes corrected sheets in the spring of 1651 in Paris. The book was printed quickly: the publisher Andrew Crooke worked from a complete manuscript, and used two printers.

Hobbes seems to have sent a fair copy of the manuscript of *Leviathan* to Charles, probably a vellum presentation copy. But some of the Anglican clergy in Paris, opposed to Hobbes's pragmatism, persuaded Charles that the book contained 'Principles of Atheism' and views prejudicial to the Church. Hobbes, once Charles's mathematics tutor, was denied access to his presence and denounced to the ecclesiastical authorities: he left Paris doubtful of his safety. Returning to London, he became reconciled to the Council of State.[7]

Printer

The printer was Andrew Crooke (1632–74), son of William Crooke, a husbandman. Apprenticed to Roger Potts, a London bookseller, Andrew was a Freeman of the Stationers' Company from 1629. He became an experienced bookseller in both London and Dublin, said to be able to read and even write in Latin. His shop was latterly at the sign of the Green Dragon in St Paul's Churchyard, and after the fire of London near Devereux Court in the Strand. In Dublin his shops were near the Castle Bridge and at the Greyhound in Castle Street. He sold plays, including some by Jonson, and Beaumont and Fletcher.

Crooke published several books of importance, notably the first edition of Sir Thomas Browne's *Religio medici* (1643) and Hobbes's *Briefe of the Art of Rhetorique* (1637), a translation from Aristotle's *Rhetoric*. Hobbes probably had frequent contacts with him before leaving England in 1640. Crooke

---

[7] For a fuller account, see Hobbes, *Leviathan*, ed. Malcolm, i. 91–100.

Fig. 15. Thomas Hobbes, *Leviathan*, heads version, BL MS Egerton 1910. Courtesy of the British Library.

allowed people to read Hobbes's manuscripts in his shop, and even to buy copies of them.[8]

Designers

The presentation drawing (Fig. 15), in which the body of Leviathan is composed of human heads facing outwards (BL, MS Egerton 1910), is almost certainly by the French etcher Abraham Bosse. This attribution was made in Bosse's lifetime and accepted by French authorities. Another attribution, to Wenceslas Hollar, supported by F. A. Borowsky in 1898 and recently by Keith Brown, is carefully considered by Noel Malcolm but rejected.[9] In the engraved, printed version, the body of the colossus is composed of full-length figures with their backs to the viewer. In all likelihood the eventual design was the result of collaboration between Hobbes and Abraham Bosse: they stayed a few minutes' walk from each other in Paris.

[8] Hobbes, *Leviathan*, ed. Malcolm, i. 92; Mark Goldie, in *ODNB*; *STC* 3.
[9] Hobbes, *Leviathan*, ed. Malcolm, i. 132–3; Keith Brown, 'Visualizing Hobbes', in Erik Tonning (ed.), *Sightings: Selected Literary Essays* (New York: Peter Lang, 2008), 177–81.

ÆSOP's
FABLES
With his Life
In English French & Latine.
The English by Tho. Philipott Esq:
The French and Latine
by Rob. Codrington M.A.
Illustrated with
one hundred and ten
SCULPTURES.
By Francis Barlow.
And
Are Sold at his House
The Golden Eagle
In New-Street,
near Shoo-Lane.
1665.

Francis Barlow
AESOP'S FABLES
1666

The beast fable, as ancient as literature itself, was already old in Hesiod's fable of the hawk and the nightingale. In Archilochus' first Epode the fable of the fox and the eagle was already applied in argument. And Phaedrus (*c.*15 BC–*c.* AD 50) versified fables of the legendary Aesop so successfully they have remained popular—even with children and even when they introduce political allusions.

Barlow's predecessors

French developments of the genre had a comparable range—from epic enlargement in the *Roman de Renart* to political observation in the fables of Marie de France (late twelfth century) and classicizing in the *Fables* of La Fontaine (1621–95). In Scotland, meanwhile, the *Moral Fabillis of Esope* moralized by Robert Henryson (*c*.1425–*c*.1508) contributed mock-heroic humour. So popular was the beast fable that versions of Aesop were among the first books printed in both England and Scotland.[1]

Francis Barlow's immediate predecessors in the illustration of the beast fable were Gheeraerts, Cleyn, and Hollar. Franz Klein or Francis Cleyn (1582–1658) illustrated Barlow's *Paraphrases of Aesop* (1651), the first of a series of increasingly splendid volumes of beast fables. In 1665 the entrepreneur John Ogilby published *The Fables of Aesop Paraphrased in Verse*, a luxury folio printed by Thomas Roycroft (fl. 1637–77). Roycroft was appointed King's Printer in oriental languages, probably in recognition of his work on the London Polyglot Bible (1655–7), a venture that involved cutting new oriental types.

For the illustration of his 1665 *Aesop* Ogilby enlisted his old colleague Wenceslaus Hollar (see previous section). Hollar's brief—in these, his first essays in illustrating imaginative literature—was to perform his usual alchemy on the base metal of Cleyn's unexciting illustrations. From his study of Marcus Gheeraerts and other beast specialists, Hollar was easily able to improve on Cleyn. The fire of London destroyed the sheets (but not the plates) of the 1665 edition, so that Ogilby was able to reprint it as *Aesopics: or a Second Collection of Fables Paraphrased in Verse* (1668).

Barlow's contribution

Like the emblem, the beast fable slipped easily across cultural borders. It was natural for Barlow to aim at a multilingual Aesop. The result was *Aesop's Fables: With his Life. In English French and Latin* (1666). For this ambitious volume Barlow employed two prolific and versatile writers, Thomas Philipot (d. 1682) and Robert Codrington (1601/2–65?). Philipot, who wrote the English text, graduated MA of Clare College, Cambridge, in 1636. Codrington, who produced the French and Latin versions of the Fables, graduated MA of Magdalen College, Oxford, in 1626. He published many translations, all with hopeful dedications to people he did not know. In 1641 he was imprisoned for a poem sympathetic to the earl of Strafford.

[1] e.g. Caxton's *Reynart the Foxe* (1481) and *Aesop's Fables* (1484); Henryson's *Moral Fables* (Edinburgh, 1571).

In the 1687 edition of his *Aesop's Fables* Barlow discarded Philipot's summaries and substituted two-couplet summaries and one-couplet 'morals' by the celebrated writer Aphra Behn (1640–89), whose style was a good deal more engaging and fashionable.

Artist

Francis Barlow (*c*.1626–1704) was probably from Lincolnshire. He was apprenticed in London to the portrait painter William Shepherd, and lived near The Drum in Drury Lane. Six of Barlow's natural history paintings survive at Clandon Park, Surrey, and two overdoors at Ham House, Surrey. In 1666 his address was The Golden Eagle in New Street, near Shoe Lane.

Barlow stood out as the best animal artist of his time. His work is distinguished by a scientific accuracy based on long study of both living and dead models. Unusually for his time, he preferred to draw animals in their natural settings, whether landscape or farmyard. Unusually, too, he had the ability to capture movement in his drawings, if not always in his prints. A good example of his strengths can be seen in the frontispiece of the second, 1687 edition of the *Fables*, which shows a thoughtful Aesop standing among his animals, with a ram nuzzling his knee. The scene suggests a domesticated Peaceable Kingdom, except that the lion looks worried.

The facing title page with its magnificent baroque frame was also Barlow's own invention. He animated the usual oval cartouche by having it supported by a selection of beasts from the fables.[2]

Tableau

The beasts selected for the title page resulted from no casual choice. Each one is linked with one of the others in a fable of Aesop: the lion and the boar, for example. More strikingly, each is paired with the fox. The wily fox featured in the fable of the lion and the fox, the wolf and the fox, the leopard[3] and the

[2] Edward Hodnett, *Francis Barlow: First Master of English Book Illustration* (Oakland, CA: University of California Press, 1978); Sheila O'Connell, in *ODNB*.
[3] Not tiger, as Hodnett, *Francis Barlow*, 168.

fox, and the boar and the fox. The most ancient allusion is to the fable of the eagle and the fox, which as we have seen appeared in Archilochus. It seems in keeping with the nature of Aesop's world that the protagonist of Barlow's title page is the smallest and most unobtrusive of the six animals. The fox is the animal looking directly at Aesop. Besides the moral values of the eagle, it probably serves as an allusion to Barlow's workplace.

Booksellers

Between 1666 and the reprint of 1677, Barlow handed over the selling of the edition to Ann Seile (whose shop was beside St Dunstan's in Fleet Street) and Edward Powell (whose shop was at the White Swan, Little Britain). For the second edition of 1687, Barlow continued as publisher but sold through other booksellers: Christopher Wilkinson (Seile's successor, at the Black-boy near St Dunstan's); Thomas Fox in Westminster Hall; and Henry Faithorne at The Rose in St Paul's Churchyard, bookseller to the Royal Society. Some of these choices may have been matters of convenience: Blackfriars, St Paul's Churchyard, and Little Britain, for example, were all near to Shoe Lane.

Printers

William Godbid (fl. 1656–1679), an important publisher and printer, printed the 1666 edition. Godbid's workplace was near the Anchor Inn in Little Britain. The printer of the second, 1681, edition was Henry Hills, senior (c.1625–88/9). Hills was notorious in the 1640s for his refusal to take sides: he printed Leveller tracts and the *Eikon basilike*. Through Cromwell he gained a monopoly on printing bibles; yet in 1677 he became the King's Printer and in 1687 Warden of the Stationers' Company. His workplace was at Ditchside in Blackfriars.

CÆLIQVE VIAS ET SIDERA MONSTRAT.

THE SPHERE
of
M. MANILIVS
made
An English
POEM
by
Edward Sherburne, Esq.

NATVRÆ VNIVERSITAS.

W. Hollar fecit 1673

VNIVERSITATIS INTERPRES

Edward Sherburne

THE SPHERE OF M. MANILIUS
1675

Marcus Manilius (fl. early first century AD) intended the *Astronomica* to rival Virgil's *Georgics*. The tone of its Stoic hymns to the divine order of creation strongly contrasts with the Epicureanism of Lucretius. Manilius' hexameter exposition of astronomy and astrology is in five books, most of which have survived. It has been edited by three great Latin scholars: Joseph Scaliger (1540–1609), Richard Bentley (1662–1742), and A. E. Housman (1859–1936). Housman affected to have a low opinion of the *Astronomica*, saying 'Manilius writes on astronomy and astrology without knowing either'—a view inconsistent with the monumental labours he devoted to Manilius from 1903 to 1930. Besides, his account of Manilius' astrology is inferior to Scaliger's.

Some modern scholars have joined with Thomas Creech in mocking Manilius for the 'vanity' that led him to choose so rebarbative a subject.[1] But the *Astronomica* was rightly admired by earlier, Renaissance scholars for offering an intelligible treatment of the ancient macrocosm. Among other valuable achievements, Manilius expounded the system of twelve tutelary guardians (2.433–52): Minerva, Venus, Apollo, Mercury, Jupiter, Ceres, Vulcan, Mars, Diana, Vesta, Juno, and Neptune. These twelve protectors, their attributes, and powers were correlated with the zodiacal signs in a different way from the now more familiar Ptolemaic scheme. In Manilius, 'Virgo with her sheaf belongs to Ceres', whereas in Ptolemy Virgo belongs to Mercury.

The Manilian scheme lay behind much of the iconography and astronomical imagery of Elizabethan art and literature. Perhaps Pythagorean in origin, it was used by Edmund Spenser for *The Faerie Queene* (1590).[2]

Author

Sir Edward Sherburne (bap. 1618–1702) was the twin son of the Secretary of the East India Company. His schoolmaster was the formidable classical scholar Thomas Farnaby. Sherburne travelled in France 1640–1, but was called back by his father's terminal illness. He succeeded to the office of Commissary General of Ordnance, and served Charles I at the battle of Edgehill.

Among Sherburne's friends were Thomas May, Thomas Randolph, Robert Herrick, Thomas Carew, and especially James Shirley and Thomas Stanley—all Royalists except the first. After Charles's execution, Sherburne shared Stanley's retirement in Hertfordshire, where he studied European poetry and wrote *Poems and Translations* (1651). It was a great age of translation, partly because translation was less dangerous politically (the classical tradition offered common ground). But translation was also a highly competitive part

---

[1] For some recent views on Manilius and Sherburne, see *OHLTE* ii. 249–50, 270–2; *OHLTE* iii. 193–4.

[2] See Alastair Fowler, *Spenser and the Numbers of Time* (London: Routledge & Kegan Paul, 1964), 65.

of literature. A. E. Housman, and following him F. J. van Beeck, thought less of Sherburne's work because it contained little original writing; but translations were themselves original. The substantial fragment of his translation of Lucretius' *De natura* compares favourably with Lucy Hutchinson's translation of the same work. At first Sherburne attempted only short pieces; later he engaged with such major challenges as Seneca's tragedies and Manilius' *Astronomica*.

As tutor to Sir John Coventry, Sherburne travelled throughout Europe in 1655–9; during this period he began his Manilius. Thus, his translation of the first book of the *Astronomica* as *The Sphere of Manilius Made an English Poem* (1675) was a long time in preparation. Even its first, incomplete version appeared only in 1673. The reason was largely shortage of funds: it took legal action to regain the office he was entitled to, and he never received more than a tenth of its emoluments. Still, the Ordnance Office was a meeting place of astronomers, and in its environment Sherburne's grasp of Manilius developed as would hardly have been possible elsewhere. The Royal Society welcomed *The Sphere*, and in 1682 he was knighted.

Artist

Wenceslaus Hollar (1607–77) was born in Prague, Bohemia, the son of an official in the land registry. His father was knighted by Rudolph II in 1600 and given the right to bear arms. But the family were Protestants, and under the new emperor, Ferdinand II, they had to convert or emigrate. Against his father's wishes, Hollar made himself an artist: in 1631 he worked for Matthäus Merian at Frankfurt am Main. Hollar's first major production was a set of views from Prague to the Netherlands, published by Abraham Hogenberg of Cologne. At Cologne, too, Hollar met the earl of Arundel, there on an embassy to the emperor. Arundel thought Hollar etched 'with a pretty spirit', and became his active patron from 1636 to 1642.

But from the start Hollar courted other patrons in England: it was not long before sets of his prints were being collected—*The Several Costumes of English Women* (1640), for example, and female figures as the four seasons (1643, 1644). His many topographical prints included the *Long View of London from the Bankside* (1647). After a spell in Antwerp, Hollar had by early 1652 returned to London, where he was employed chiefly by antiquarians such as John Ogilby, Sir William Dugdale, and Elias Ashmole.

In 1660 Hollar hoped a large-scale map of London would make him less needy financially. But the fire of London in 1666 dashed this hope. Ever since 1642, when his patron Arundel left for exile in Italy, Hollar had always had to work too much—and at only 12d. per hour. The result was a huge output, which counted against his reputation. Pennington's *Catalogue* lists over 2,700 etchings alone.[3]

Hollar's early work showed the influence of Dürer, Beham, and Aegidius Sadeler. His pre-eminence was slow to become apparent. With the advantage of hindsight, however, one can see that Hollar came to be a magisterial etcher, technically quite the equal of Rembrandt. His visual record of the age—various, detailed, truthful, objective—has no rival.

His connection with Sherburne was of long standing. Twenty years before Hollar etched the second title page of *The Sphere of Manilius*, he had worked on a dedicatory inscription to Sherburne—EDWARDO SHERBORN ARMIGERO—for John Ogilby's luxury edition of Virgil, which boasted forty-three prints wholly by Hollar after drawings by Francis Cleyn.

Hollar had an equable, serene disposition, only occasionally disturbed by passions. He married twice: in 1641 to Margaret Tracy (d. 1653), a servant of the countess of Arundel; and in 1656 to Honora Roberts. He died a Roman Catholic.

Tableau

The persons of the tableau are easily identified; yet each has subtleties. Urania crowned with seven stars reclines on clouds substantial enough to merge with the similarly shaped mountains. With her R hand she supports a tablet inscribed THE SPHERE OF M. MANILIUS MADE AN ENGLISH POEM. BY EDWARD SHERBURNE, ESQ. With her L she holds a telescope—a novel attribute—through which she looks at seven stars, one of them much brighter than the others.

---

[3] Richard Pennington, *A Descriptive Catalogue of the Etched Work of Wenceslaus Hollar 1607–77* (Cambridge: Cambridge University Press, 1982).

Below and to the L is a winged Pan standing on a plinth with an inscription identifying him as the 'totality of nature'. In his L hand he holds the *syrinx* or seven-reeded pipe of Pan: in his R a shepherd's crook, showing him as the god of flocks. He has the legs, thighs, tail, and hooves of a goat. His hairy legs were supposed to indicate his earthiness. His loose clothing is embroidered: the upper garment with stars, the lower with a topography of rivers, mountains, and buildings. These were probably borrowed from Cartari's and Alciati's portrayals of Pan and Jupiter. Pan's unclassical wings are doubtless from the same Renaissance illustrations.[4]

Below Urania and to the R is Hermes (Mercury), Pan's father, identifiable by his *petasus* or winged cap, by his winged heels, and by the winged caduceus in his R hand. An ingenious god of probing intellect, Hermes was a mystagogue who with his staff dispelled the clouds of obscurity.[5] In his L hand he lightly touches a lyre, by tradition seven-stringed.[6] He was the patron of lettered enquiry and interpretation (*hermeneia*): Boccaccio called Mercury *interpres secretorum*.[7]

Between Pan and Hermes, an armillary sphere rests on the earth in a gap in the plinth.

Inscriptions

1. On a scroll above Urania's head: CAELIQUE VIAS ET SIDERA MONSTRAT ('may the Muse show me heaven's pathways, the stars', Virgil, *Georgics* 2.477). The Virgilian context is relevant, implying as it does that Manilius, too, may be thought of as a priest of the Muses: 'But as for me— first above all, may the sweet Muses whose holy emblems, under the spell of a mighty love, I bear, take me to themselves, and show me heaven's pathways, the stars, the sun's many lapses, the moon's many labours.'[8]

---

[4] Vincenzo Cartari, *Imagini delli dei de gl'antichi* (1556; facsimile edn, ed. Walter Koschatzky, Graz: Akademische Druck, 1963), 72; Natale Conti, *Mythologiae* (Padua, 1616; facsimile edn, ed. Stephen Orgel, New York: Garland, 1979), 247.

[5] Edgar Wind, *Pagan Mysteries in the Renaissance*, rev. edn (London: Faber, 1967), 122.

[6] Manilius, *Astronomica* 5.324–38.   [7] Wind, *Pagan Mysteries*, 123.

[8] Virgil, *Georgics* 2.477.

2. On the plinth beneath Pan: NATURAE UNIVERSITAS ('the totality of nature').

3. On the plinth beneath Mercury: UNIVERSITATIS INTERPRES ('interpreter of the universe').

Chronogram

The first of the inscriptions contains a chronogram of 1675, the date of Hollar's second etched title page for the first complete edition of Sherburne's translation: CAEL|IQVE VIAS SID|ERA MONSTRAT (CLVSSDM = MDCLXXV). Only letters in initial or final positions of a word or word stem are available; and SS = XX by substitution.

Designers

Probably Sherburne and Hollar worked together, at least in the initial stages. Several blank layouts surviving among Hollar's papers show he had experience of such work.

Publisher

Nathaniel Brooke worked at the Sign of the Angel in Cornhill, near the Royal Exchange. He was a popular bookseller–publisher: in 1663 his catalogue comprised eighty-nine titles already in print and twenty-six ready for printing.

Here in the rich, the honour'd, fam'd and great,
See the false scale of Happiness complete!

Published by J.&P. Knapton Feb. 6th 1744.

Alexander Pope
AN ESSAY ON MAN
1745

In Pope's time there was a vogue for pictures of classical ruins, in which the superhuman scale of the architecture often dwarfed the staffage. The art of Giambattista Piranesi (1720–78) was after all coeval with the poetry of Pope. The real historical remains of the Roman Empire, for centuries converted and reinhabited but now crumbling, posed large questions about the brevity of human grandeur—as did the medieval ruins left over from the dissolution of the monasteries. Many poems meditated on this theme. Indeed, the fascination with ruins was so great that historical ruins became insufficient to meet the demand, and artificial ruins were built as retro-Gothic features of some modern estates. These new–old ruins sometimes betrayed their romantic inspiration by the hermits paid to act as their custodians.[1]

---

[1] Paul Frankl, *The Gothic: Literary Sources and Interpretations through Eight Centuries* (Princeton: Princeton University Press, 1960), index, s.v. *ruins*; Nick Groom, *The Gothic: A Very Short Introduction* (Oxford: Oxford University Press, 2012), 60, 77, *et passim*.

Ruins aroused diverse associations and reflections, perhaps most obviously the transience of human culture. A prominent motif in scenes of Gothic ruin was dismemberment, as in the architectural *capriccio* favoured by artists of the Ricci family.[2] Headless statues abounded—echoes, doubtless, of Reformation iconoclasm. Later, ruins seem to have had more ambivalence: their very incompleteness opened up opportunities for replacement or new building.[3] Pope's frontispiece suggests all these associations.

Tableau

Tombs, ruins, and emblematic objects are illuminated from the top R. In the upper register the 'mouldering stones' of a 'towering pyramid'[4] or obelisk is linked to a tree by a large cobweb. Below, ranged L to R, can be distinguished the dismembered statue of an *imperator* wearing Roman military uniform and proudly standing on a plinth; a guttering candle and laureate skull resting on a sarcophagus—which in turn rests on another plinth supporting a musical score and a flute or recorder; a broken column; an old man blowing bubbles beside a fountain pouring onto the ground from a grotesque head; and a vista of the Roman Colosseum.

By Pope's time, emblems had lost their former obscurity and were easily accessible to many viewers. The musical score and instrument outlasting the musician; the philosopher of the fountain; and the smoke and bubble of vanity: these were not hard to understand.[5]

Inscriptions

1. VIRO IMMORTALI ('to an immortal man'), on the plinth of the dismembered Roman statue.

---

[2] Benjamin Boyce, 'Baroque into Satire: Pope's Frontispiece for the "Essay on Man"', *Criticism*, 4 (1962), 18.

[3] Thomas McFarland, *Romanticism and the Forms of Ruin* (Princeton: Princeton University Press, 1981), index, s.v. *incompleteness*.

[4] James Thomson, 'To the Memory of Sir Isaac Newton' (1727), lines 174–5, in *The Complete Poetical Works*, ed. J. Logie Robertson (London: Oxford University Press, 1908), 441.

[5] Huston Diehl, *An Index of Icons in English Emblem Books 1500–1700* (Norman, OK, and London: University of Oklahoma Press, 1986), 39.

2. SIC TRANSIT GLORIA MUNDI ('so passes away the glory of the world'), on a sarcophagus. Perhaps deriving from a similar sentence in the *De imitatione Christi* 1.3 of Thomas à Kempis (1379–1471), the sentence was used during the ceremony of enthroning a new pope. It was pronounced at the moment when flax was ignited as a symbol of the transitoriness of earthly grandeur.

3. CAPITOLI IMMOBILE SAXUM ('the Capitol's motionless bedrock', *Aeneid* 9.448), on the plinth of the column. The words allude to an authorial eulogy of Nisus and Euryalus encapsulating the essence of Rome in the Capitoline hill that corresponded to Latinus' city. Benjamin Boyce remarks the irony of 'immobile' on a 'mostly vanished column'.[6]

4. ROMA AETERNA ('unalterable Rome'), the commonplace of Rome as *urbs aeterna* overprinted on the ruined Colosseum with similar irony.

5. A. POPE INVT (*invenit*, 'designed this'), on a stone slab in the lower L corner.

6. As epigraph to the whole frontispiece: HERE IN THE RICH, THE HONOUR'D, FAM'D AND GREAT | SEE THE FALSE SCALE OF HAPPINESS COMPLETE! (*An Essay on Man*, 4.269–308), a passage surveying 'the lofty and famous men whose grandeur and wealth have rested, like Venice, on dirt and seaweed and whose "trophy'd arches" and proud palaces sheltered guilt and unhappiness'.[7]

7. Below the epigraph comes the imprint: PUBLISHED BY J. AND P. KNAPTON, FEB. 6TH 1744.

Moralization

The frontispiece is a tomb picture, then a familiar genre.[8] Marco Ricci's *Varia* series had similar architecture and emblematic objects: obelisks, monuments, and statues of great leaders.[9] Literary counterparts included John Dyer's *Ruins of Rome* (1740) and James Hervey's *Meditations* (1746). William

---

[6] Boyce, 'Baroque into Satire', 20.

[7] Ibid. 22, comparing Pope's *Temple of Fame* (1715), lines 352–3, a warning to ambitious fools—'Your Statues moulder'd, and your Names unknown'.

[8] Boyce, 'Baroque into Satire', 23, 25, on Sebastiano and Marco Ricci.

[9] Ibid. 21.

Warburton's prefatory *Advertisement* before *An Essay on Man* rightly takes the general import of the frontispiece to be the transience of fame and glory.[10] It expressed 'the Vanity of human Glory, in the false pursuits after Happiness: Where the Ridicule, in the Curtain-cobweb, the Death's-head crowned with laurel, and the several Inscriptions on the fastidious [i. e. proud; magnificent] ruins of Rome, have all the force and beauty of one of his best wrote Satires'.

Pope's frontispiece, however, may have had a more particular meaning. The published version of *An Essay* invites the reader to consider such as Julius Caesar (4.258), Francis Bacon, and 'Cromwell, damn'd to everlasting fame' (4.284). But a manuscript revision made the Duke of Marlborough the main subject of Pope's attack on grandiose heroes:

> Mark by what wretched steps Great ** grows,
>
> From dirt and sea-weed as proud Venice rose;
>
> One equal course how Guilt and Greatness ran,
>
> And all that rais'd the Hero and the Man.
>
> Now Europe's Laurels on his brows behold,
>
> But stain'd with Blood, or ill exchang'd for Gold.[11]

Pope had been offered by the Duchess 'a very considerable sum' if he 'inserted a good character of the Duke, and absolutely refused it'.[12] Hence the verse: 'In vain his consort bribes for venal song'.[13] Pope suppressed the revision when the Duchess changed her political orientation and he no longer wished to offend her. He told Joseph Spence: 'I have omitted a character,

---

[10] William Warburton (1698–1779), lawyer, controversialist, and from 1759 bishop of Gloucester, was Pope's editor and literary executor. He defended the orthodoxy of *An Essay on Man*. A good friend to Pope, he fought in the culture wars of the time against Voltaire, David Hume, and John Wesley. Warburton achieved fame with *The Divine Legation of Moses* (1737–41).

[11] Pope, 'A Character', in Alexander Pope, *Poems*, ed. John Butt et al., 11 vols in 12 (London: Methuen; New Haven: Yale University Press, 1939–69) (the 'Twickenham Pope'), vi. *Minor Poems* (New Haven and London, 1964), 358–9; Maynard Mack (ed.), *The Last and Greatest Art: Some Unpublished Poetical Manuscripts of Alexander Pope* (Newark: University of Delaware Press; London and Toronto: Associated University Presses, 1984), 199.

[12] Joseph Spence, *Observations, Anecdotes and Characters of Books and Men*, ed. James M. Osborn, 2 vols (Oxford: Clarendon Press, 1966), i. 161–2, quoting Warburton.

[13] Pope, 'A Character', line 28, in 'Twickenham Pope', vi. 358.

though I thought it one of the best I had ever written, of a very great man, who had everything from without to make him happy, and yet was very miserable from the want of virtue in his own heart.' Although Pope 'did not say who this was, but mentioned Julius Caesar and the late King of Sardinia as instances of a like kind', Spence correctly inferred that Pope meant Marlborough.[14]

Writing to Francis Atterbury on 27 July 1722 about the Duke's vast funeral,[15] Pope told him that 'at the time of the Duke of Marlborough's funeral, I intend to lye at the Deanery, and moralize one evening with you on the vanity of human Glory'.

Warburton draws attention to some of the emblems in the frontispiece, such as the fountain running to waste, and the bearded Philosopher blowing bubbles with a straw, which is taken to represent the vanity of Scholastic philosophy—using artificial logic to invent 'airy arguments in support of false science' while human understanding 'is suffered to lie waste and uncultivated'.

Designer

Warburton's *Advertisement* attributes the frontispiece illustration to Pope himself, as does the inscription on the stone slab. But, as Boyce explains, matters may not be so simple. Two earlier versions of the illustration exist: a red chalk drawing by Pope (once in the possession of William Mason) and a sepia drawing inscribed AUCTOR IPSE INVT & I. M. DELINEAVIT ('the author himself designed this and I.M. drew it'). Probably Pope drew the chalk sketch and I.M. developed this in the sepia drawing. But who was I.M. (or J.M.)? Boyce weighs the claims of J. Mynde, Major, I. Mason, and James Miller—all designers or engravers associated with Pope and Warburton— without deciding on any one. He supposes that the engraver omitted the Latin inscription below the sepia drawing. But in fact one can just discern, with the help of magnification, the inscription A. POPE INVT.

---

[14] Spence, *Observations, Anecdotes and Characters*, i. 162.
[15] Alexander Pope, *The Correspondence*, ed. George Sherburn, 5 vols (Oxford: Clarendon Press, 1956), ii. 127. The Duke's funeral took place on 9 August 1722.

Printers

The printers were John Knapton (bap. 1696, d. 1767–70) and Paul Knapton (bap. 1703, d. 1755). Their father James Knapton (d. 1736) was a leading London bookseller, John being apprenticed to him 1712–19. Paul, however, was apprenticed to Arthur Butterworth 1721–8. The brothers opened new premises at the Crown, Ludgate Street. John having co-published Pope's letters in 1737, Pope recommended him to Warburton in 1741; their eventual alliance led to Warburton's edition of Pope's *Works*. The Knaptons also published Samuel Johnson's *Dictionary* in 1746, but Paul died in that year. John became bankrupt, although the debts were largely paid off by sale of copyrights. He subsequently continued to publish in a more limited way.

PUBLII VIRGILII

MARONIS

BUCOLICA,

GEORGICA,

ET

AENEIS.

BIRMINGHAMIAE:

Typis JOHANNIS BASKERVILLE.

MDCCLVII.

John Baskerville
VIRGIL'S BUCOLICA, GEORGICA ET AENEIS
1757

There have been many famous Virgils, some distinguished for their editing, like Joseph Scaliger's (Antwerp, 1575), and some for their translation, like Gavin Douglas's (1553) or John Dryden's (1697). Others are noted
for their illustrations—for example, the stylish Vatican Virgil and the provincial, primitive, Roman Virgil;[1] the manuscript Virgil commissioned by
Petrarch with Simone Martini's great frontispiece;[2] Sebastian Brant's 1502

---

[1] John Harthan, *The History of the Illustrated Book: The Western Tradition* (London:
Thames & Hudson, 1981), 14; David H. Wright, *The Roman Vergil and the Origins of Medieval
Book Design* (London: British Library, 2001).

[2] Christopher de Hamel, *A History of Illuminated Manuscripts* (1996; rev. edn, London:
Phaidon, 1997), pl. 214.

Virgil with its medieval woodcuts, and John Ogilby's 1653 Virgil with its engravings by Wenceslaus Hollar. But, among English Virgils, one of the most important is sloppily edited and without illustrations.

This is John Baskerville's 1757 Virgil, published in Birmingham, which announced the revival of English typography.[3] Before Baskerville, William Caslon (1693–1766) dominated English type foundry, but, although his standards were high, his conservative style did little to advance typography. English typography remained provincial, as if content to follow Netherlandish fashions. This changed dramatically after Baskerville's royal quarto Virgil (Birmingham, May 1757), his folio Bible (Cambridge, 1763), and his *Orlando furioso* (Birmingham, 1773).[4] On the continent, Baskerville's work was admired by Pierre-Simon Fournier and especially by Giambattista Bodoni (1740–1813), printer to the Count of Parma from 1768.[5] Bodoni turned away from Fournier's rococo typography to the plainer neoclassicism of Baskerville. In Scotland, too, Baskerville's ideals inspired Douglas and Foulis, as in their Horace (Glasgow, 1756).[6] And John Bell and William Bulmer joined the movement, initiating the type-foundry style of 'modern' types that was to dominate in the nineteenth century.[7] Even William Pickering (1796–1854), remembered as reviving Caslon's types and ornaments, also used Baskerville's types.

In England, however, Baskerville was far from displacing Caslon. Opinion there was very mixed. Among typographical experts such as Talbot Baines Reid, Baskerville had its admirers; but William Morris thought it 'uninteresting'.[8] Printers and public alike remained satisfied with their Caslon imitations. From time to time, however, papers appreciative of Baskerville appeared on both sides of the Atlantic, from 1899 to 1914. Then in 1921 Frederic Warde adopted a Baskerville fount for Princeton University Press and Bruce Rogers for Harvard. In 1923 Monotype recut and regularized Baskerville, and in the following year this version was acquired by Cambridge University Press, which used it as a standard book type. Monotype Baskerville at last brought the design into popular use.

---

[3] Stanley Morison and Kenneth Day, *The Typographic Book 1450–1935* (London: Ernest Benn, 1963), 46–9: no. 209.

[4] Ibid., no. 216.   [5] Ibid. 47.   [6] Ibid., no. 199.   [7] Ibid. 48.

[8] Stanley Morison, *A Tally of Types: With Additions by Several Hands*, ed. Brooke Crutchley (1953; Cambridge: Cambridge University Press, 1973), 81–7.

Typography

Baskerville aimed at a purer, more geometrically constructed typography, and at perfection of the individual letters, which he had cut by John Handy (1720?–92/3).[9] This neoclassical style depended on simple elegance, undecorated except for an occasional printed rule. Its effect was impressively monumental, if a little bleak and cold. Baskerville's types had a great difference in thickness between horizontal and vertical elements—more vertical axis than Caslon's. And they had serifs at right angles with the strokes.[10] Baskerville's wide spacing and dramatic expanses of white were influential but extravagant, particularly in the large formats he preferred. His continental imitators followed him in the proportions of print and spaces, but retained the narrow-bodied letters favoured by Fournier (1712–68).

The effects of Baskerville's revolutionary typography were enhanced by his use of very white wove papers, hot-pressed. These minimized the sense of paper quality, in favour of simple contrasts of black and white.

Printer

John Baskerville (1707–75) began as a professional writing master, cutting gravestone inscriptions and teaching penmanship: Matthieu Lommen refers to him as 'the eccentric English writing master'.[11] After inheriting his father's estate in 1738, he manufactured japanned metal wares, accumulating a fortune. From 1750, when he began printing, he oversaw the cutting of his types, and experimented with ink and paper. His wide spacing and striking letter forms eventually brought about a revolution in English typography. But in his lifetime his publications, although widely influential, made little profit.[12]

---

[9] Mathieu Lommen, *The Book of Books: 500 Years of Graphic Innovation* (London: Thames & Hudson, 2012), 174–5, 208.

[10] Ibid. 174.   [11] *OCB* i. 509.

[12] Lommen, *Book of Books*, 208; Morison, *Tally of Types*, 81–7.

THE ROSE AND THE RING;

OR, THE

HISTORY OF PRINCE GIGLIO AND PRINCE BULBO.

A Fireside Pantomime for Great and Small Children.

BY MR. M. A. TITMARSH

(W. M. THACKERAY),

Author of "Vanity Fair," "The Newcomes," "Henry Esmond," "English Humorists,"
"Pendennis," "The Great Hoggarty Diamond," &c.

NEW YORK:

HARPER & BROTHERS, PUBLISHERS,

FRANKLIN SQUARE.

1855.

William Makepeace Thackeray
THE ROSE AND THE RING
1855

To write *The Newcomes*, Thackeray fled the temptations of London and his ex-mistress Mrs Brookfield by travelling on the Continent with his two daughters. In Germany, Switzerland, and France he finished six of the novel's twenty-four monthly parts, before moving to Rome in December 1853. Robert Browning found an apartment for him at the Palazzo Poniatowski. His spacious lodgings were immediately above the Spillmans, famous pastry-cooks—a location highly agreeable to Thackeray's daughters Anne (aged 16) and Minny (13). They were able to entertain friends among the English colony: the Brownings, Fanny Kemble, William Welmore Story the sculptor, and other families with children. Extravagant parties featuring cakes celebrated Twelfth Night in the traditional way.

At home, such cakes would have taken the form of English Twelfth Night characters or their symbols—King, Queen, and royal regalia; Lady, Lover, Dandy, Captain; and Sir Gregory Goose and Sir Tunbelly Clumsy. But in Rome these traditional English figures were not to be had; so to supply their absence Thackeray drew them in watercolour, with a few additional inventions.

In December Thackeray had suffered from malarial fever. But when he recovered in January 1854 he managed to complete two more numbers of his novel, besides adding to the 'fairy tale' he was working round the pictures he drew to amuse a sick child, Edith Story, also convalescing from malarial fever. In March, now living in Naples, he told the story to his own daughter Anne, who was in bed with scarletina, and to Minny when she too caught it. (Young people used then to spend much of their lives in bed with fevers.) Even when Thackeray himself went down with gastric fever, he would shuffle out of bed in his slippers to see to the young ones and continue the story. By now he had decided to make his fairy tale mock-epic into a Christmas Book—light fiction with seasonable content. The characters began to acquire ramifying associations. The King became Valoroso and the Queen 'Mrs Valoroso'; Lover and Lady were Giglio and Angelica (who shared her name with the heroine of *Orlando furioso*); and the Captain was Count Kutassoff Hedsoff. New inventions kept being added: a French cook Marmitanio, a court physician Dr Pildrafto, and Squaretoso the Chancellor of Paflagonia. For these, Thackeray drew on *Commedia dell' arte* figures such as Il Dottore, and of course on pantomime. The Christmas Book version was in draft by October 1854.

Thackeray invited comparison with Charles Dickens, who had made the Christmas Book his own, putting some of his best work, however rapidly done, into its unambitious form—the *Christmas Carol* (1843); *A Christmas Tree*; *The Holly-Tree*; and more. Perhaps in rivalrous mood, Thackeray too dashed off a series of Christmas Books in a realistic mode, from *Mrs Perkins' Ball* (1846) to *The Kickleburys on the Rhine* (1850). *The Rose and the Ring* (1855) was the last of these; but Thackeray chose for it a pantomimic mode: the ugly Countess Gruffanuff is pure pantomime Dame.

In adapting the story to Christmas Book requirements, he had to make many cuts. Fairy Hopstick went; although Fairy Blackstick (perhaps for her name's associations) was kept, to tell of her boredom with the fairy trade after thousands of years.[1] Drawings too were cut: out of eighty two, only fifty-five were selected. As Thackeray juggles different genres of comedy and farce and

[1] Black Rod is the Gentleman Usher responsible for maintaining order in the House of Lords.

satire—now with burlesque moralizing, now with hyperbolic chivalry—*The Rose and the Ring* is full chiefly of his characteristic quality: pure fun. He has a lightness of touch Dickens never quite reached. For adult readers, meanwhile, there is satire of hidebound monarchy and didactic morality. And for the children, such delights as never quite knowing when the geography is real or improvised. Was there really a Princess of Crim Tartary?

Versions

In the 1855 edition, the illustrations are disappointing. Much of the original brio was lost through bad engraving for print. So now there are two very different versions of *The Rose and the Ring*: the painted and the printed. Of these, the manuscript is better by far, as regards the illustrations. Its watercolour drawings are almost as fresh as those that delighted Edith Story and Anne and Minny. It survives, and has been printed as *The Rose and the Ring… Reproduced in Facsimile from the Author's Original Illustrated Manuscript in The Pierpont Morgan Library. With an Introduction by Gordon N. Ray* (1947).[2]

The frontispiece of the 1855 edition uses a standard, three-part layout of title in the uppermost register; a vignette centred; and author and imprint below. The title in five lines (four of Roman capitals, one black letter) is THE | ROSE AND THE RING; | OR, THE | HISTORY OF PRINCE GIGLIO AND PRINCE BULBO. | A FIRE-SIDE PANTOMIME FOR GREAT AND SMALL CHILDREN. The vignette shows the fireside pantomime enjoyed by five 'great and small children' grouped on either side of the fire, between their mother (L) and grandmother (R), with a cat centre front.

The pantomime itself is imagined in the fire; recalling Coleridge's 'Frost at Midnight'. There, a film fluttering in the 'low burnt fire', is made 'a companionable form, | Whose puny flaps and freaks the idling Spirit | By its own moods interprets […] | And makes a toy of Thought'.[3] In Thackeray's frontispiece the

---

[2] (New York: Pierpont Morgan Library and Spiral Press, 1947). Our Frontispiece 14 is from this manuscript.

[3] Poem 171 in Samuel Taylor Coleridge, *Poetical Works*, ed. J. C. C. Mays, 2 vols (Princeton: Princeton University Press, 2001), i. 453–4, lines 14–16, 19–22 (*Collected Works*, xvi).

film becomes a knight on horseback, so that the fire-cum-stage serves as a doorway to *The Rose and the Ring*.

In the lowest register, the author is given as MR M. A. TITMARSH (Thackeray's usual *nom de guerre*), AUTHOR OF 'THE KICKLEBURYS ON THE RHINE', 'MRS PERKINS'S BALL', &C. &C.—listing two of Thackeray's latest Christmas Books. The imprint comes last: LONDON: | SMITH, ELDER, AND CO., 65, CORNHILL. | 1855.—Or, in the US edition, NEW YORK: | HARPER & BROTHERS, PUBLISHERS, | FRANKLIN SQUARE. | 1855.

Artist and Illustrator

Thackeray (1811–63) was his own illustrator. When he had thrown away much of his fortune, and lost most of the rest through bank failures in India, Thackeray attempted to make a living as a painter, and later as an illustrator. He illustrated his own books brilliantly, particularly *Vanity Fair* (1847–8). He ranked among the best illustrators of his time, although his lack of formal

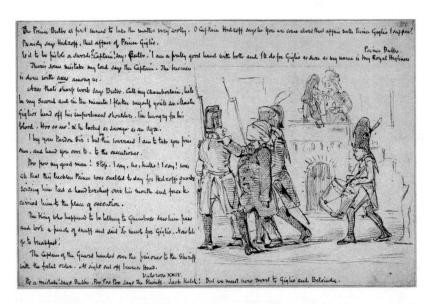

Fig. 16. Bulbo arrested, William Thackeray, *The Rose and the Ring*: autograph manuscript: Rome, 1853, fo. 51ʳ. The Pierpont Morgan Library, New York. MA 926. Purchased by J. P. Morgan, Jr, 1915.

Fig. 17. Prince Bulbo, William Thackeray, *The Rose and the Ring*: autograph manuscript: Rome, 1853, fo. 36ʳ (detail). The Pierpont Morgan Library, New York. MA 926. Purchased by J. P. Morgan, Jr, 1915.

training sometimes conceals this. His chief faults were in draughtsmanship (which is best learnt early); in etching he was able to learn much from George Cruikshank.[4] Even so, his uncertainty with the etching needle made for disastrously ambiguous instructions to the wood-engraver.

Yet Thackeray's text and illustrations, at their best, are intimately related in a harmonious marriage of picture and story—so much so that the illustrations to *The Rose and the Ring* could be said, for example, to offer the best evidence for a life of Bulbo (Figs 16 and 17). Not only was Thackeray one of the finest illustrators of his age, but, among self-illustrators (one thinks of Lewis Carroll and Mervyn Peake and J. R. R. Tolkien), he is probably supreme in any age.

Like some other works intended for double readerships—*Treasure Island*, for instance—*The Rose and the Ring* has an elusive, inexhaustible quality. Perhaps this is because no reader can ever be two ages at the same time, at once.

---

[4] John Harthan, *The History of the Illustrated Book: The Western Tradition* (London: Thames & Hudson, 1981), 202.

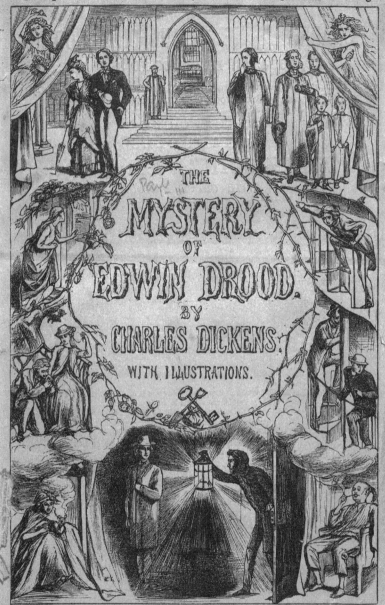

THE MYSTERY OF EDWIN DROOD.

BY CHARLES DICKENS.

WITH ILLUSTRATIONS.

LONDON: CHAPMAN & HALL, 193, PICCADILLY.

Advertisements to be sent to the Publishers, and ADAMS & FRANCIS, 59, Fleet Street, E.C.

[The right of Translation is reserved.]

Charles Dickens
THE MYSTERY
OF EDWIN DROOD
1870

Few novels have attracted so much controversy as *The Mystery of Edwin Drood*. In large part this is because Charles Dickens died in 1870, leaving his last novel unfinished. We have only six of its monthly parts—about half of the intended novel. In consequence *Drood* has become a mystery in a way never intended by the author. Quite apart from uncertainty about how the unwritten parts might have turned out, there is an inherent mystery in the parts extant, a deliberate mysteriousness Dickens preserved as long as he could, even when instructing the book's illustrators. It is not surprising that readers differ about the story, being always halfway through it.

Was John Jasper to have murdered his nephew, or only to have harboured death wishes? Was someone else the murderer? Or did Edwin somehow survive a murder attempt and then go into hiding? Such questions are reflected in the title-page illustrations. Indeed, the illustrators are among our chief sources of information about Dickens's plans for the unwritten parts. After all, he had to ensure that the illustrations did not contradict text still to be written.

Many questions about the continuation of the plot were once thought to be resolved by the definite statements of John Foster, Dickens's friend and biographer. But serious doubts have since been cast on Foster's reliability. It is hardly an exaggeration to say that interpretation of the title page comes close, in this unusual instance, to interpretation of the novel itself.

Tableau

The general arrangement of scenes from the novel is typically Gothic. It is in a retrospective style recalling medieval art and the memorial title pages of the seventeenth century. There are three rows of vignettes. The lower corners present the opium den of Chapter 1 (where Jasper may have expressed evil thoughts) overheard by Princess Puffer (L) and the Chinaman (R). The billowing opium smoke separates this row or level from the next above, where it merges with the larger obscurity of the novel. Between these corner figures is the dramatic lantern-lit scene, which does not correspond with any in the novel as we have it. The lantern scene has been taken to show Jasper entering a room in which he is surprised to encounter Edwin.[1] Is he surprised that Edwin should still be alive?

The middle level of the tableau corresponds to the stage of the narrative during which Edwin is missing. At upper L, Rosa looks towards a scroll inscribed LOST; at lower L a kneeling Jasper declares his love to Rosa. At centre middle, framed in a double wreath, is the title: THE MYSTERY OF EDWIN DROOD BY CHARLES DICKENS WITH ILLUSTRATIONS. Below the title but still within the wreath is an emblem of crossed key and spade with Durdles's dinner bundle. R of the title a vignette shows three figures

---

[1] Charles Dickens, *The Mystery of Edwin Drood*, ed. Margaret Cardwell (Oxford: Clarendon Press, 1972), 241; W. W. Robson, 'The Choir-Master and the Single Buffer: An Essay on *The Mystery of Edwin Drood*', in Colin Gibson (ed.), *Art and Society in the Victorian Novel: Essays on Dickens and his Contemporaries* (London: Macmillan, 1989), 53.

ascending a spiral staircase. The leading figure, in Charles Collins's view, is Jasper 'unconsciously pointing an accusing finger at himself in the top picture'.[2]

In the uppermost register are two corner figures set off by curtains. The L figure has flowers in her hair, and holds a posy of flowers. Representing virtuous love and defying gravity, she reclines on the curtain. The opposing figure on the R has serpents in her dishevelled hair, and holds a dagger in her R hand. According to a convention of long standing, she personifies hate and envy.[3] With her L hand she draws back the curtain to reveal the principal scene.

Between the contrasting personifications, on the same upper level, is the apparently placid world of the ancient cathedral close. In the exact centre the 'low arched cathedral door' is open, showing the altar. By the door stands the verger, Mr Tope. To the L, beside Virtuous Love, Edwin and Rosa walk arm in arm in mutual amity, although Rosa's face is averted. On the R, next to Hatred, a group of choristers process: one of them, evidently Jasper, gazes intensely at the happy couple.

The façade of the cathedral shows it to be Gothic; and indeed Cloisterham at large has vestiges of Gothic too: it is 'a city of another and a bygone time':

Fragments of old wall, saint's chapel, chapter-house, convent, and monastery, have got incongruously or obstructively built into many of its houses and gardens, much as kindred jumbled notions have become incorporated into many of its citizens' minds. All things in it are of the past.[4]

Artists

Charles, Wilkie Collins's brother, the first illustrator chosen, worked on *Drood* for four months, but had to give up because of ill health. He communicated valuable comments on Dickens's plans for the novel, especially in a letter to Daly:

---

[2] Charles Dickens, *The Mystery of Edwin Drood*, ed. Margaret Cardwell, World's Classics (1982; Oxford: Oxford University Press, 2009), p. xii.

[3] See, e.g., Cesare Ripa, *Iconologia* (Padua, 1611; facsimile edn, New York and London: Garland, 1976), 262, 525.

[4] Dickens, *Drood*, ed. Cardwell (1972), 14.

It was intended that Jasper himself should urge on the search after Edwin Drood and the pursuit of his murderer, thus endeavouring to direct suspicion from himself, the real murderer. This is indicated in the design, on the right side of the cover, of the figures hurrying up the spiral staircase emblematical of a pursuit. They are led on by Jasper who points unconsciously to his own figure in the drawing at the head of the title.

The second illustrator was Samuel Luke Fildes (1844–1927). At first, Fildes practised the new style of illustration associated with Millais.[5] But Dickens probably chose Fildes for his social realism, as in his famous design 'Houseless and Hungry' for the *Graphic* (1869).[6] Though admired by Van Gogh, Fildes's work moved away from illustration and towards journalism—a widespread tendency at the time because of costs. Some of his best work was in the monthly parts of *Drood*, where he shows himself at one with Dickens's text.[7]

As wood-engravers at this date, the Dalziels might have expected to be chosen; but Fildes explicitly asked for Ebenezer Landells (1808–60). Landells, a founder of *Punch*, had been apprenticed to Thomas Bewick, and was considered one of the best living wood-engravers.[8]

[5] See John Harvey, *Victorian Novelists and their Illustrators* (London: Sidgwick & Jackson, 1970), 160.

[6] See Gordon Ray, *The Illustrator and the Book in England from 1791 to 1914* (Oxford: Pierpont Morgan Library and Oxford University Press, 1976), 98.

[7] See Paul Goldman, *Victorian Illustration: Pre-Raphaelites, the Idyllic School and the High Victorians* (Menston: Scolar, 1996; repr. Aldershot and Burlington, VT: Lund Humphries, 2004), 239.

[8] See Harvey, *Victorian Novelists*, 161, 195; Amanda-Jane Doran, *ODNB*.

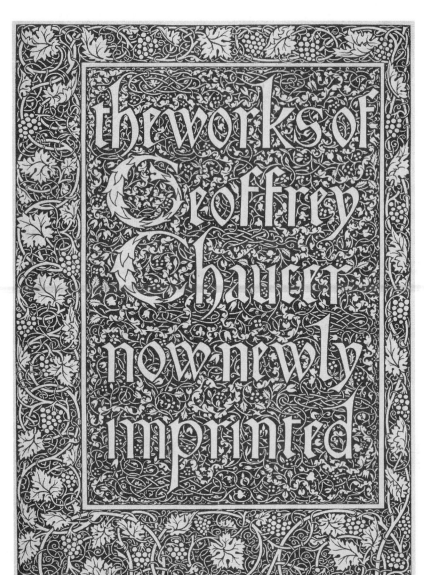

the works of Geoffrey Chaucer now newly imprinted

Geoffrey Chaucer
WORKS
1896 (The Kelmscott Chaucer)

The Kelmscott Chaucer has been described as 'one of the finest books ever produced'.[1] It was also a strategic contribution to the history of book production, looking back as it did to the late medieval book, as well as forward to what might replace the mass-produced book of Morris's own time. By its example it firmly established the idea that the material book could be beautiful: that all books had aesthetic qualities, good or bad.

Designer

The main designer was William Morris (1834–96), author, socialist, and visionary of European prominence. The son of a London financier, Morris was able

[1] *OCB* ii. 842.

to act on his feelings in an innocently simple way. Together with his friend Edward Burne-Jones, he stood against the visual ugliness of industrialized manufacture, and was determined to reintroduce aesthetic values. As early as 1861 he had formed a decorating company focused on the domestic arts, whose status he determined to raise. The Firm produced furniture, wallpaper, and textiles for institutions and wealthy patrons. It was so successful that it played a major part in the Arts and Crafts movement, sharing its opposition to the automatic processes of mass production.

Morris naturally gravitated into the Pre-Raphaelite circle with its pursuit of idealized medievalism. Influenced by the reformist ideas of Ruskin, Carlyle, and Charles Kingsley, Morris's thinking became more political: in 1883 he joined the Democratic Federation, a Marxist socialist party, and in the next year the anti-Parliamentarian splinter group, the Socialist League.[2]

The Kelmscott Press

In 1891 Morris set up his own printing firm, the Kelmscott Press, at Kelmscott Manor, near Lechlade on the Gloucestershire–Oxfordshire border. Here he pursued his idea of printing on a pre-industrial hand press. He used intense black ink and handmade linen-based paper from Kent. And he even cast his own types emulating fifteenth-century models: Jensen's roman Golden; the black-letter Troy; and a reduced version of Troy called Chaucer. These were all cut by Edward Prince. The illustrations and borders were printed from the wood in limited editions aimed at rich patrons and collectors.

Morris's designs were internationally admired and imitated—by the Doves press and the Ashendene in Britain, and in the USA by Bruce Rogers (1870–1937). The private press movement generally, however different its vision, owed much to Morris. Perhaps most important, Stanley Morison (1889–1967) applied some of Morris's ideas to commercial book production. Morison used many historical types, and was anti-modernist; but he had a more practical, less visionary approach. Where he differed most from Morris was in his conviction that printing should not be noticed. It should be invisible, or rather transparent to readers.[3]

[2] Fiona MacCarthy, *ODNB*.   [3] *OCB* ii. 944.

Artist

Sir Edward Coley Burne-Jones (1833–1898) was the son of a framer and gilder. He was educated at King Edward's school, Birmingham, and Exeter College, Oxford, where he met William Morris, who was also intended for holy orders. After touring northern France with Morris in 1855, Burne-Jones decided on a career in art. For a time he attended an art school, but left it for informal instruction by Rossetti, who had a strong influence on him. Soon he was working for Rossetti on murals for the debating chamber of the Oxford Union. Earlier, he had designed but later almost disowned a steel-engraved frontispiece and title page for Archibald Maclaren's *The Fairy Family* (1857). This early work influenced other young artists but proved to be incompatible with his own later Pre-Raphaelite style.

In 1860, Burne-Jones married Georgiana Macdonald: their circle included Morris, Rossetti, and John Ruskin, a strong critic and fine draughtsman. Visits to Italy in 1859 and 1862 enlarged Burne-Jones's vision and conceptions of art; but his lack of professional training led to harsh criticism of any paintings he exhibited.

A decisive phase of Burne-Jones's development was his work for an illustrated edition of Morris's. As many as 300 woodcuts were planned, and Burne-Jones produced a great many drawings; but the project for an illustrated volume was eventually abandoned. Nevertheless, Burne-Jones contributed a title-page illustration for the 1868 *The Earthly Paradise* (the block for which was probably cut by Morris himself). And he had learned to become a productive illustrator. In the peaceful obscurity of illustrative art he thrived. He won many commissions for narrative paintings, although he still shrank from public exhibitions and the consequent attacks on his unconventional style.

Burne-Jones's idea that pictures could tell a story ran counter to official assumptions; and his overtly sexual images were not always acceptable in the exhibition room. Inevitably there came a breach with Ruskin in 1871. Burne-Jones continued, however, to work for the Morris firm. In the end he had contributed designs for as many as thirteen Kelmscott Press books.[4]

---

[4] Paul Goldman, *Victorian Illustration: Pre-Raphaelites, the Idyllic School and the High Victorians* (1996: London: Lund Humphries, 2004), 11–12.

The Kelmscott Chaucer

In production from 1892 to 1896, the Kelmscott Chaucer has eighty-seven illustrations after Burne-Jones's designs, eighteen frames, fourteen borders, thirty-six principal initial words or letters, and many smaller initials. Morris designed all this, but Burne-Jones drew them in pencil: Richard Catterson-Smith enhanced the drawings: and they were rendered as wood-engravings by W. H. Hooper (familiar from his work for William Small).[5]

Stanley Morison saw Morris's Chaucer as the culmination of the archaistic experiments of William Pickering and A. W. Pugin. He speaks of the 'spec-tacular gothic picturesqueness' of the Kelmscott Chaucer, and describes it as 'the most lavishly decorated piece of typography of the whole post-medieval period'.[6] In direct contrast to Baskerville, Morris longed for decoration: 'the Kelmscott Chaucer is splendid in its conception, magnificent in its decoration, defiant in its archaism and scrupulous in its execution.'[7] This magisterial achievement claimed the attention of collectors and created a market for fine books produced outside the industrial process. Morris was at the heart of the private press movement with its aesthetic objectives.

On the one hand, Morris restored the woodcut to its former pre-eminence; and he did almost as much for calligraphy. He was not concerned with com-mercial printing by machines—although he might use modern methods (such as photography) where they solved a particular problem. Sir Nikolaus Pevsner and other modernist critics tried to claim Morris for modernism,[8] and he has since been more often placed as a conservative radical designer. But someone so original and eccentric is hard to locate on any cultural map. 'Still in quantity production a hundred years after his death', he is 'arguably the most successful industrial designer ever known'.[9]

---

[5] Goldman, *Victorian Illustration*, 141; *OCB* ii. 842.

[6] Morison, in Stanley Morison and Kenneth Day, *The Typographic Book 1450–1935* (London: Ernest Benn, 1963), 14, 16.

[7] Ibid. 50.

[8] See William S. Peterson, *The Kelmscott Press: A History of William Morris's Typographical Adventure* (Berkeley and Los Angeles: University of California Press, 1991).

[9] MacCarthy, *ODNB*.

GLOSSARY

Cartouche: an escutcheon in the form of a paper or parchment scroll with the ends curled over. As an element of title-page architecture, it usually bore an inscription giving the author, title, or IMPRINT. See Marjorie Corbett, 'The Cartouche in English Engraving', *Motif*, 10 (1963), 61.

Chronogram: an inscription in which some letters express, by their numerical values, a date—often the date of publication. In overt chronograms the operative letters are often capitalized; but in covert chronograms the operative letters are determined by rules governing their availability. See Introduction: Chronograms; also James Hilton, *Chronograms Continued and Concluded [...] A Supplement* (1885).

Colophon: an inscription at the end of an early book, giving the imprint, often with decorative typography. Later, the colophon was replaced by an imprint on the title page. See Theodore Low de Vinne, *A Treatise on Title-Pages with Numerous Illustrations in Facsimile and some Observations on the Early and Recent Printing of Books* (1902).

Device, or *impresa*: an emblematic figure or 'conceit', expressed pictorially and accompanied by a motto. The device was adopted by a person or family as a heraldic or quasi-heraldic bearing. See Dan Russell, *The Emblem and Device in France* (1985).

Ecphrasis, Ecphrastic: a description of a work of art. Ecphrastic writing sometimes attempts to conjure up a picture by acting on several senses. See Jean Hagstrum, *The Sister Arts* (1958).

Elogy: an inscription explaining a portrait, often eulogizing the subject or describing the sitter's character.

Emblem: a fable or allegory suggesting a symbolic picture. Typically, emblems were gathered together into emblem books. Each emblem might have three or four elements: the title, LEMMA, or MOTTO; the picture; the EPIGRAM; and an explanatory passage in verse or prose. But the explanation might be merged with the epigram or omitted altogether. And in the case of 'nude' emblems the picture might be left to the imagination. Emblems had a wider application than DEVICES:

193

their general truths were meant to stimulate moral reflection. See John Manning, *The Emblem* (2002).

Epigram: ancient Greek epigrams of many kinds were later gathered in the enormous *Greek Anthology*. In Latin, Martial specialized in erotic and scurrilous epigrams. Renaissance epigrams were poems on any subject, varying in length from a distich to several hundred lines. They were classified as *fel* (gall), *acetum* (vinegar), *sal* (salt), *mel* (honey), and *foeditas* (foul)—that is, bitterly satiric, sour or sharp, funny, sweetly amorous, and foul. All were to be witty and pointed. More recently, epigrams have tended to be very short, aiming at brilliant wit as in those of Oscar Wilde or J. V. Cunningham. See Rosalie Colie, *The Resources of Kind* (1973).

Epigraph: an inscription on a building or a title page, usually a quotation. Sometimes epigraphs concealed a CHRONOGRAM.

Frontispiece: the façade of a building, or one of its pediments. Later, the title page or PARATEXT of a book. In modern usage, an illustration facing the title page.

Impresa: see DEVICE.

Imprint: information as to the publisher's name and the place and date of publication. The imprint is usually placed at the foot, or on the back, of the title page.

Incipit: in the Middle Ages the incipit (Latin, 'beginneth') functioned as a text's title. In elaborately decorated manuscripts such as *The Book of Kells*, a familiar incipit was often presented cryptically, using scrambled and multilingual lettering. See Jesse M. Gellrich, *The Idea of the Book in the Middle Ages* (1985), and Bernard Meehan (ed.), *The Book of Kells* (2012).

Lemma: the subject or argument of an EMBLEM.

Motto, Mot: a word or phrase expressing a general reflection or ideal; a pithy maxim.

Paratext: all that precedes the text itself. Sometimes it is taken to include the preface and introduction.

Pegma, **Pegme:** the temporary framework or scaffolding of Renaissance street theatre, royal entries, and triumphal celebrations. See George Kernodle, *From Art to Theatre: Form and Convention in the Renaissance* (1944).

Rebus: the rebus (Latin, 'by things') uses words or pictures to represent parts of word (often syllables). The names of the things sound the same as the syllables. So *Grafton* might be expressed by pictures of a *graft* and a *tun* or barrel. See Jean Céard and Jean-Claude Margolin, *Rébus de la Renaissance: Des images qui parlent* (1987), or Tony Augarde, *The Oxford Guide to Word Games* (1984).

Strapwork: a decorative motif originating in the work of Rosso Fiorentino and the School of Fontainebleau. It led to a form of CARTOUCHE, using three-dimensional leather instead of parchment or paper.

Symbolum (**Latin 'symbol'**): an early term for EMBLEM. See John Manning, *The Emblem* (2002).

Tableau: a group of allegorical, mythological, or literary personages (or their statues), posed in a frontispiece or title page. Their characteristic costumes and attributes summarize the topics of the book, offering ready-made aides-mémoires. See Frances Yates, *The Art of Memory* (1966).

BIBLIOGRAPHY

[Place of publication is London, unless otherwise stated.]

Achilleos, Stella, ' "Ile bring thee *Herrick* to *Anacreon*": Robert Herrick's Anacreontics and the Politics of Conviviality', in Ruth Connolly and Tom Cain (eds), *'Lords of Wine and Oile': Community and Conviviality in the Poetry of Robert Herrick* (Oxford: Oxford University Press, 2011), 191–219.

Agrippa, Cornelius, *De occulta philosophia libri tres*, ed. Vittoria Perrone Compagni (Leiden: Brill, 1992).

Alciati, Andrea, *Emblematum liber* (Augsburg: Steyner, 1531).

Alciati, Andrea, *Emblematum libellus* (Venice: Aldus, 1546).

Alciati, Andrea, *Emblemata cum commentariis* (Padua: Pietro Paolo Tozzi, 1621; facsimile edn, New York and London: Garland, 1976).

Alexander, Jonathan J. G., *The Painted Page: Italian Renaissance Book Illumination 1450–1550* (New York: Prestel, 1994).

Alexander, Michael, *The Middle Ages in Modern England* (New Haven: Yale University Press, 2007).

Allison, A. F., and Goldsmith, V. F. (eds), *Titles of English Books*, 2 vols (Folkestone: Dawson, 1976).

Anderson, Flemming G., et al. (eds), *Medieval Iconography and Narrative: A Symposium* (Odense: Odense University Press, 1980).

Ariosto, Lucovico, *Ludovico Ariosto's* Orlando Furioso *Translated into English Heroical Verse by Sir John Harington (1591)*, ed. Robert McNulty (Oxford: Clarendon Press, 1972).

Armstrong, Elizabeth, *Robert Estienne: Royal Printer* (Cambridge: Cambridge University Press, 1954).

Augarde, Tony, *The Oxford Guide to Word Games* (Oxford: Oxford University Press, 1984).

Bacon, Francis, *Sylva sylvarum: Or a Natural Historie. In Ten Centuries* (London: W. Rawley, 1627).

Bacon, Francis, *The* Instauratio magna, *Part II:* Novum organum *and Associated Texts*, ed. Graham Rees with Maria Wakely, *The Oxford Francis Bacon*, xi (Oxford: Clarendon Press, 2004).

Bath, Michael, *Renaissance Decorative Painting in Scotland* (Edinburgh: National Museums of Scotland Publishing, 2003).

Bath, Michael, and Russell, Daniel S. (eds), *Deviceful Settings: The English Renaissance Emblem and its Contexts*, Selected Papers from the Third International Emblem Conference, Pittsburgh, 1993 (New York: AMS, 1999).

Bennett, J. A. W. (ed.), *Selections from John Gower* (Oxford: Clarendon Press, 1968).

Blair, Ann, *The Theater of Nature: Jean Bodin and Renaissance Science* (Princeton: Princeton University Press, 1997).

Blayney, Peter W. M., *The Stationers' Company and the Printers of London 1501–1557*, i: *1501–1546*; ii: *1547–1557* (Cambridge: Cambridge University Press, 2013).

Blunt, Anthony, *Art and Architecture in France 1500 to 1700*, Pelican History of Art (Pelican, 1953; rev. edn, New Haven, Yale University Press, 1999).

Boccaccio, Giovanni, *Genealogy of the Pagan Gods*, trans. Jon Solomon, I Tatti Renaissance Library (Cambridge, MA: Harvard University Press, 2011), i.

Boissard, A. I. I., *Emblemata* (Frankfurt, 1596).

Bolzoni, Lina, *The Gallery of Memory: Literary and Iconographic Models in the Age of the Printing Press*, trans. Jeremy Parzen. Toronto Italian Studies (Toronto: University of Toronto Press, 2001).

Bond, Donald F. (ed.), *The Spectator*, 5 vols (Oxford: Clarendon Press, 1965).

Bourne, Claire M. L., '"High Design": Beaumont and Fletcher Illustrated', *English Literary Renaissance*, 44 (2014), 275–327.

Boyce, Benjamin, 'Baroque into Satire: Pope's Frontispiece for the "Essay on Man"', *Criticism*, 4 (1962), 18.

Bremmer, Jan, and Roodenburgh, H. (eds), *A Cultural History of Gesture* (Ithaca, NY: Cornell University Press, 1991).

Brown, Keith, 'Visualizing Hobbes', in Erik Tonning (ed.), *Sightings: Selected Literary Essays* (New York: Peter Lang, 2008), 177–81.

Bungus, Petrus, *Numerorum mysteria ex abditis plurimarum discipliarum fontibus hausta* [...] (Bergamo: Venturi, 1591).

Burton, Robert, *The Anatomy of Melancholy*, ed. J. B. Bamborough, Thomas C. Faulkner, et al., 6 vols (Oxford: Clarendon Press, 1989–2000).

Bury, Michael, *The Print in Italy 1550–1620* (British Museum, 2001).

Butsch, Albert Fidelis (ed.), *Handbook of Renaissance Ornament: 1290 Designs from Decorated Books* (New York: Dover, 1969).

Calasso, Roberto, *The Art of the Publisher*, trans. Richard Dixon (Penguin Books, 2015).

Camden, William, *Britannia* (1607; Hildesheim and New York: Anglistica & Americana, 1970).

Camden, William, *Britannia*, trans. E. Gibson (1695).

Camden, William, *Remains Concerning Britain* (1605), ed. R. D. Dunn (Toronto: University of Toronto Press, 1984).

Cameron, Euan, *The European Reformation* (Oxford: Clarendon Press, 1991).

Campbell, Gordon, *Bible: The Story of the King James Version 1611–2011* (Oxford: Oxford University Press, 2010).

Carew, Thomas, *Coelum Britannicum* (1634).

Carroll, Eugene A. (ed.) *Rosso fiorentino: Drawings, Prints, and Decorative Arts.* Exhibition catalogue (Washington: National Gallery of Art, 1987).

Carlson, D., 'Woodcut Illustrations of *The Canterbury Tales*, 1483–1602', *Library*, 6th ser., 19 (1957), 25–67.

Carruthers, Mary J., *The Book of Memory: A Study of Memory in Medieval Culture* (Cambridge: Cambridge University Press, 1990).

Cartari, Vincenzo, *Imagini delli dei de gl'antichi* (1556; facsimile edn, ed. Walter Koschatzky, Graz: Akademische Druck, 1963).

Cauchi, Simon, 'The "Setting Foorth" of Harrington's Ariosto', *Studies in Bibliography*, 36 (1983), 137–68.

Cave, Roderick, and Ayad, Sara, *A History of the Book in 100 Books* (British Library, 2014).

Caxton, William, *Selections from William Caxton*, ed. N. F. Blake (Oxford: Clarendon Press, 1973).

Céard, Jean, and Margolin, Jean-Claude, *Rébus de la Renaissance: Des images qui parlent*, 2 vols (Paris: Maisonneuve and Larose, 1986).

Chandler, Alice, *A Dream of Order: The Medieval Ideal in Nineteenth-Century English Literature* (Lincoln, NE: University of Nebraska Press, 1971).

Cheles, Luciano, *The Studiolo of Urbino: An Iconographical Investigation* (University Park, PA: Pennsylvania State University Press, 1986).

Cheshire, Paul, ' "I lay too many Eggs": Coleridge's "Ostrich Carelessness" and the Problem of Publication', *Coleridge Bulletin*, NS 23 (2004), 1–25.

Clements, Robert J., *Picta Poesis*, Temi e Testi, 6 (Rome: Edizioni di storia e letteratura, 1960).

Cloud, Random, 'From Tranceformations in the Text of *Orlando Furioso*', *Library Chronicle of the University of Texas at Austin*, 20 (1990), 60–85.

Cohen, Jane Rabb, *Dickens and his Original Illustrators* (Cambridge, MA: Harvard University Press, 1968).

Coleridge, Samuel Taylor, *Poetical Works*, ed. J. C. C. Mays, 2 vols (Princeton: Princeton University Press, 2001) (*Collected Works*, xvi).

Colie, Rosalie, *The Resources of Kind: Genre-Theory in the Renaissance* (Berkeley and Los Angeles: University of California Press, 1973).

Combe, Thomas, *The Theatre of Fine Devices* (R. Field, 1614).

Connolly, Ruth, and Cain, Tom (eds), *'Lords of Wine and Oile': Community and Conviviality in the Poetry of Robert Herrick* (Oxford: Oxford University Press, 2011).

Conti, Natale, *Mythologiae* [. . .] (Padua, 1616; facsimile edn, ed. Stephen Orgel, New York: Garland, 1979).

Cooper, John, *The Queen's Agent: Francis Walsingham at the Court of Elizabeth I* (Faber, 2011).

Cooper, Thomas, *Thesaurus linguae Romanae et Britannicae* (1578; facsimele edn, Hildesheim and New York: Olms, 1975).

Corbett, Marjorie, 'The Architectural Title-Page', *Motif*, 12 (1964), 48–62.

Corbett, Marjorie, 'The Cartouche in English Engraving', *Motif*, 10, ed. Ruari McLean (Shenval, 1962), ch. 5.

Corbett, Marjorie, and Lightbown, R. W., *The Comely Frontispiece: The Emblematic Title-Page in England 1550–1660* (Routledge & Kegan Paul, 1979).

Cowie, A. P., *The Oxford History of English Lexicography*, 2 vols (Oxford: Clarendon Press, 2009).

Crashaw, Richard, *The Poems*, ed. L. C. Martin (Oxford: Clarendon Press, 1927).

Crystal, David, *Begat: The King James Bible and the English Language* (Oxford: Oxford University Press, 2010).

Curtius, Ernst Robert, *European Literature and the Latin Middle Ages*, trans. Willard R. Trask (Routledge & Kegan Paul, 1953).

Daniel, Samuel, *The Worthy Tract of Paulus Jovius, Contayning A Discourse of Rare Inventions, Both Militarie and Amorous Called* Imprese (London: Hardpress, n.d.).

Daniell, David, *The Bible in English* (New Haven and London: Yale University Press, 2003).

Davies, Hugh William, *Devices of the Early Printers 1457–1560* (Grafton, 1935).

Davies, John, *The Poems*, ed. Robert Krueger (Oxford: Clarendon Press, 1975).

Debus, Allen, *The English Paracelsians* (New York: Watts, 1966).

Dickens, Charles, *The Mystery of Edwin Drood*, ed. Margaret Cardwell (Oxford: Clarendon Press, 1972).

Dickens, Charles, *The Mystery of Edwin Drood*, ed. Margaret Cardwell, World's Classics (1982; Oxford: Oxford University Press, 2009).

Diehl, Huston, *An Index of Icons in English Emblem Books 1500–1700* (Norman, OK, and London: University of Oklahoma Press, 1986).

Disraeli, Isaac, *Curiosities of Literature*, 3 vols, rev. edn (Warne, 1881).

Dobranski, Stephen, *Readers and Authorship in Early Modern England* (Cambridge: Cambridge University Press, 2005).

Donaldson, Ian, *Ben Jonson: A Life* (Oxford: Oxford University Press, 2011).

Drayton, Michael, *The Works*, ed. J. William Hebel, 5 vols (Oxford: Shakespeare Head Press, 1931–41).

Dryden, John, *The Poems*, iv. *1693–1696*, ed. Paul Hammond and David Hopkins (Harlow: Pearson, 2000).

Dryden, John, *Of Dramatic Poesy and Other Critical Essays*, ed. George Watson, 2 vols (Dent, 1962).

Dryden, John, *A Discourse Concerning Satyre*, ed. George Watson (Dent, 1962).

Elvin, Charles Norton, *A Dictionary of Heraldry* (Kent, 1889).

Evers, Bernd, and Thoenes, Christof (eds), *Architectural Theory from the Renaissance to the Present* (Cologne: Taschen, 2003).

Fane, Mildmay, Second Earl of Westmorland, *The Poetry of Mildmay Fane: From the Fulbeck, Harvard and Westmorland Manuscripts*, ed. Tom Cain (Manchester: Manchester University Press, 2001).

Farmer, Norman K., *Poets and the Visual Arts in Renaissance England* (Austin, TX: University of Texas Press, 1984).

Farmer, Norman K., 'Herrick's Hesperidean Garden: *ut picture poesis* Applied', in R. B. Rollin and J. Max Patrick (eds), *'Trust to Good Verses': Herrick Tercentenary Essays* (Pittsburgh: University of Pittsburgh Press, 1978), 15–51.

Febvre, Lucien, and Martin, Henri-Jean, *The Coming of the Book: The Impact of Printing 1450–1800*, trans. David Gerard (Verso, 1976).

Florio, John, *Queen Anna's New World of Words* (1611; facsimile edn, Menston: Scolar, 1968).

Fowler, Alastair, *Spenser and the Numbers of Time* (Routledge & Kegan Paul, 1964).

Fowler, Alastair, *Kinds of Literature: An Introduction to the Theory of Genres and Modes* (Oxford: Clarendon Press; Cambridge, MA: Harvard University Press, 1982; repr. 1985).

Fowler, Alastair, 'The Emblem as a Literary Genre', in Michael Bath and Daniel Russell (eds), *Deviceful Settings* (New York: AMS, 1999), 1–31.

Fowler, Alastair, 'Ut Architectura Poesis', in Clare Lapraik Guest (ed.), *Rhetoric, Theatre and the Arts of Design: Essays Presented to Roy Eriksen* (Oslo: Novus, 2008), 146–71.

Foxon, David, *Pope and the Early Eighteenth-Century Book Trade*, rev. James McLaverty (Oxford: Clarendon Press, 1991).

Frankl, Paul, *The Gothic: Literary Sources and Interpretations through Eight Centuries* (Princeton: Princeton University Press, 1960).

Franken, D., *L'Œuvre gravé de van de Passe* (Amsterdam, 1881).

Fraunce, Abraham, *Symbolicae philosophiae liber quartus et ultimus*, ed. John Manning, trans. Estelle Haan (New York: AMS, 1991).

Fréart de Chambray, Roland, *Parallèle de l'architecture antique et de la moderne* [...] (Paris: Martin, 1650).

Freeman, Rosemary, *English Emblem Books* (New York: Octagon, 1978).

French, Peter J., *John Dee: The World of an Elizabethan Magus* (London: Routledge & Kegan Paul: New York: Dorset, 1989).

Gellrich, Jesse M., *The Idea of the Book in the Middle Ages* (Ithaca, NY: Cornell University Press, 1985).

Gibson, Colin (ed.), *Art and Society in the Victorian Novel: Essays on Dickens and his Contemporaries* (Macmillan, 1989).

Gilbert, Allan H., *The Symbolic Persons in the Masques of Ben Jonson* (New York: AMS, 1969).

Gillespie, Stuart, *English Translation and Classical Reception* (Oxford: Wiley-Blackwell, 2011).

Giovio, Paolo, *A Discourse of Rare Inventions, Called* Imprese, trans. Samuel Daniel (S. Waterson,1585); repr. ed. A. B. Grosart for private circulation (1896; repr. Hardpress, n.d.).

Goldman, Paul, *Victorian Illustration: Pre-Raphaelites, the Idyllic School and the High Victorians* (Menston: Scolar, 1996; repr. Aldershot and Burlinton, VT: Lund Humphries, 2004).

Golz, Hubert, *Thesaurus antiquariae huberrimus, ex antiquis tam numismatum quam marmorum inscriptionibus* [...] (Antwerp, 1579).

Grafton, Anthony, *The Culture of Correction in Renaissance Europe*. Pannizi Lecture, 2009 (British Library, 2011).

Grafton, A., Most, G. W., and Setti, S. (eds), *The Classical Tradition* (Cambridge, MA: Belknap Press, 2010).

The Grolier Club's Catalogue of Original and Early Editions of Some of the Poetical and Prose Works of English Writers from Langland to Prior, 4 vols in 1 (Holland Press, 1964).

Groom, Nick, *The Gothic: A Very Short Introduction* (Oxford: Oxford University Press, 2012).

Groot, Irene de, and Vorstman, Robert, *Maritime Prints by the Dutch Masters*, trans. Michael Hoyle (Gordon Fraser, 1980).

H.A. [Henry Hawkins], *The Devout Heart* (Rouen, 1634).

Hagstrum, Jean, *The Sister Arts: The Tradition of Literary Pictorialism and English Poetry from Dryden to Gray* (1958; Chicago: University of Chicago Press, 1968).

Hall, John, *Emblems with Elegant Figures* (1658; repr. Menston: Scolar, 1970).

Hamel, Christopher de, *A History of Illuminated Manuscripts* (1996; rev. edn Phaidon, 1997).

Hamel, Christopher de, *The Book: A History of the Bible* (New York and London: Phaidon, 2001).

Hamel, Christopher de, *Bibles: An Illustrated History from Papyrus to Print* (Oxford: Bodleian Library, 2011).

Harington, John, *Nugae Antiquae: Being a Miscellaneous Collection of Original Papers in Prose and Verse*, collected by Henry Harington, ed. Thomas Park, 2 vols (1804; repr. New York, 1966).

Harp, Richard, and Stewart, Stanley (eds), *The Cambridge Companion to Ben Jonson* (Cambridge: Cambridge University Press, 2000).

Harthan, John, *The History of the Illustrated Book: The Western Tradition* (Thames & Hudson, 1981).

Harvey, John R., *Victorian Novelists and their Illustrators* (Sidgwick & Jackson, 1970).

Hellinga, Lotte, *William Caxton and Early Printing in England* (British Library, 2010).

Herrick, Robert, *The Complete Poetry*, ed. Tom Cain and Ruth Connolly (Oxford: Clarendon Press, 2013).

Herrick, Robert, *The Complete Poetry*, ed. J. Max Patrick (1963; New York: Norton, 1968).

Hill, Sir George F., *Corpus of Italian Medals* [...] *of the Renaissance before Cellini*, 2 vols (1930); rev. and enlarged by Graham Pollard as *Renaissance Medals at the National Gallery of Art* (Phaidon Press for the Samuel H. Kress Foundation, 1967).

Hilton, James, *Chronograms Continued and Concluded* [...] *A Supplement Volume* (Elliot Stock, 1885).

Hind, Arthur M., *Engraving in England in the Sixteenth and Seventeenth Centuries*, i. *The Tudor Period*; ii. *The Reign of James I*, 2 vols (Cambridge: Cambridge University Press, 1952–5).

Hind, Arthur M., *An Introduction to a History of Woodcut* (repr. New York: Dover, 1963).

Hobbes, Thomas, *Leviathan*, ed. Noel Malcolm, 3 vols (Oxford: Clarendon Press, 2012).

Hodnett, Edward, *English Woodcuts 1480–1535* (rev. edn., Oxford: Oxford University Press, 1975).

Hodnett, Edward, *Francis Barlow First Master of English Book Illustration* (Oakland, CA: University of California Press, 1978).

Horapollo, *The Hieroglyphics of Horapollo*, trans. and ed. George Boas (New York: Pantheon, 1950).

Isaac, Frank, *English Printers' Types of the Sixteenth Century* (Oxford: Oxford University Press, 1936).

Johnson, Alfred Forbes, *A Catalogue of Engraved and Etched English Title-Pages down to* [...] *1691* (Oxford: Bibliographical Society and Oxford University Press, 1934).

Johnson, Alfred Forbes, *German Renaissance Title-Borders* (Oxford: Bibliographical Society and Oxford University Press, 1929).

Jonson, Ben, *Ben Jonson*, ed. C. H. Herford, Percy Simpson, and Evelyn Simpson, 11 vols (Oxford: Clarendon Press, 1925–52).

Jonson, Ben, *The Cambridge Edition of the Works of Ben Jonson*, ed. David Bevington et al., 7 vols (Cambridge: Cambridge University Press, 2012).

Josten, C. H., 'A Translation of John Dee's *Monas hieroglyphicum* (Antwerp, 1564)', *Ambix*, 12 (1964), 84–221.

Juel-Jensen, Bent, 'An Oxford Variant of Drayton's *Polyolbion*', *Library*, 5th ser., 16 (1961), 52–4.

Kastan, David Scott, ' "The Noise of the New Bible": Reform and Reaction in Henrician England', in Claire McEachern and Debora Shuger (eds), *Religion and Culture in Renaissance England* (Cambridge: Cambridge University Press, 1997), 46–68.

Kernodle, George R., *From Art to Theatre: Form and Convention in the Renaissance* (Chicago and London: University of Chicago Press, 1944).

Kilroy, Gerard, *The Epigrams of Sir John Harington* (Farnham and Burlington, VT: Ashgate; 2009).

King, Edmund M. B., *Victorian Decorated Trade Bindings 1830–1880* (British Library, 2003).

Kirkwood, A. E. M., 'Richard Field, Printer, 1589–1624', *Library*, 4th ser., 12 (1931–2), 1–39.

Kolve, V. A., *Chaucer and the Imagery of Narrative: The First Five Canterbury Tales* (Arnold, 1984).

Lafréry, Antoine (Antonio Lafreri), *Speculum Romanae magnificentiae* (Rome: self-published, *c.*1575).

Lagerqvist, L. O., and Dolley, R. H. M., 'The Problem of the "Fleur-de-Lis" Sceptre on the Sigtuna Coins of Cnut', *British Numismatic Journal*, 30 (1960), 57–60.

Le Grand, M., *Fabliaux or Tales, Abridged from French Manuscripts of the* XIITH and XIIITH *Centuries* (Bulmer, 1796).

Levin, Harry, 'The Title as a Literary Genre', *MLR* 72 (1977), pp. xxiii–xxxvi.

Lewis, C. S., *Studies in Medieval and Renaissance Literature*, ed. Walter Hooper (Cambridge: Cambridge University Press, 1966).

Lommen, Mathieu, *The Book of Books: 500 Years of Graphic Innovation* (Thames & Hudson, 2012).

Love, Harold, 'Scribal Publication in Seventeenth-Century England', *Transactions of the Cambridge Bibliographical Society*, 9 (1987), 130–54.

Love, Harold, *Scribal Publication in Seventeenth-Century England* (Oxford: Clarendon Press, 1993).

Luborsky, Ruth Samson, 'Connections and Disconnections between Images and Texts: The Case of Secular Tudor Book Illustration', *Word and Image*, 3 (1987), 74–85.

Luborsky, Ruth Samson, and Ingram, Elizabeth Morley, *A Guide to English Illustrated Books 1536–1603*, 2 vols (Tempe, AZ: MRTS, 1998).

McFarland, Thomas, *Romanticism and the Forms of Ruin* (Princeton: Princeton University Press, 1981).

McGann, Jerome, *A New Republic of Letters: Memory and Scholarship in the Age of Digital Reproduction* (Cambridge, MA: Harvard University Press, 2014).

Mack, Maynard (ed.), *The Last and Greatest Art: Some Unpublished Poetical Manuscripts of Alexander Pope* (Newark: University of Delaware Press; London and Toronto: Associated University Presses, 1984).

McKenzie, Donald Francis, *The London Book Trade in the Later Seventeenth Century* (Cambridge: Cambridge University Press, 1977).

McKerrow, Ronald B., *An Introduction to Bibliography for Literary Students* (Oxford: Clarendon Press, 1927).

McKerrow, R. B., *Printers' and Publishers' Devices in England and Scotland 1485–1640* (1913; Oxford: Oxford University Press for the Bibliographical Society, 1949).

McKerrow, R. B., and Ferguson, P. S., *Title-Page Borders Used in England and Scotland 1485 to 1640* (Oxford: Bibliographical Society and Oxford University Press, 1932.

McLeod, Randall (Random Cloud), 'The Fog of arr', *Leia*, 26 (2013), 163–247.

McPherson, David, 'Ben Jonson's Library and Marginalia', *Studies in Philology*, 71 (1974), 1–106.

Madan, Falconer, 'Early Representations of the Printing-Press', *Bibliographica*, 1 (1895), 223–48, 494–504.

Manning, John, *The Emblem* (Reaktion, 2002).

Marcus, Leah S., *Unediting the Renaissance: Shakespeare, Marlowe, Milton*, rev. edn (Routledge, 1996).

Meakin, H. L., *The Painted Closet of Lady Ann Bacon Drury* (Farnham: Ashgate, 2013).

Meehan, Bernard (ed.), *The Book of Durrow: A Medieval Masterpiece at Trinity College Dublin* (Dublin: Town House, 1996).

Meehan, Bernard (ed.), *The Book of Kells* (Thames & Hudson, 2012).

Miskimin, Alice, 'The Illustrated Eighteenth-Century Chaucer', *Modern Philology*, 77 (1979), 26–55.

Moore, Helen, and Reid, Julian (eds), *Manifold Greatness: The Making of the King James Bible* (Oxford: Bodleian Library, 2011).

Morison, Stanley, *A Tally of Types: With Additions by Several Hands*, ed. Brooke Crutchley (1953; Cambridge: Cambridge University Press, 1973).

Morison, Stanley, and Day, Kenneth, *The Typographic Book 1450–1935* (Ernest Benn, 1963).

Mortimer, Ruth (ed.), *French Sixteenth-Century Books*, 2 vols (Cambridge, MA: Belknap, 1964).

Mortimer, Ruth (ed.), *Italian Sixteenth-Century Books*, 2 vols (Cambridge, MA: Belknap, 1974).

Myers, Robin, Harris, Michael, and Mandelbrote, Giles (eds), *Owners, Annotators and the Signs of Reading* (British Library, 2006).

Nash, Andrew (ed.), *The Culture of Collected Editions* (Palgrave, 2003).

Nesbitt, Alexander (ed.), *200 Decorative Title-Pages* (New York: Dover, 1964).

Newdigate, Bernard H., *Michael Drayton and his Circle* (Oxford: Blackwell for the Shakespeare Head Press, 1961).

Norton, David, *A Textual History of the King James Bible* (Cambridge: Cambridge University Press, 2005).

Onians, John, *Bearers of Meaning: The Classical Orders in Antiquity, the Middle Ages, and the Renaissance* (Princeton: Princeton University Press, 1988).

Ong, Walter J., SJ, *Ramus, Method, and the Decay of Dialogue* (Cambridge, MA: Harvard University Press, 1958).

Orgel, Stephen, 'Jonson and the Arts', in Richard Harp and Stanley Stewart (eds), *The Cambridge Companion to Ben Jonson* (Cambridge: Cambridge University Press, 2000), 140–51.

Papworth, J. W., *An Alphabetical Dictionary of Coats of Arms* (Richards, 1874).

Paradin, Claude, *Devises heroïques* (Lyons, 1557), ed. Alison Saunders (Menston: Scolar, 1989).

Parry, Graham, *The Golden Age Restored: The Culture of the Stuart Court, 1603–42* (Manchester: Manchester University Press, 1981).

Parry, Graham, 'Ancient Britons and Early Stuarts', in Robin Headlam Wells, Glenn Burgess, and Rowland Wymer (eds), *Neo-Historicism: Studies in Renaissance Literature, History and Politics* (Cambridge: D. S. Brewer, 2000), 155–78.

Peacham, Henry, *Peacham's Compleat Gentleman* (1634), ed. G. S. Gordon (Oxford: Clarendon Press, 1906).

Pearsall, Derek, *The Life of Geoffrey Chaucer: A Critical Biography* (Oxford: Blackwell, 1992).

Pelikan, Jaroslav, *The Reformation of the Bible: The Bible of the Reformation* (New Haven: Yale University Press, 1996).

Pennington, Richard, *A Descriptive Catalogue of the Etched Work of Wenceslaus Hollar 1607–77* (Cambridge: Cambridge University Press, 1982).

Peterson, William S., *The Kelmscott Press: A History of William Morris's Typographical Adventure* (Berkeley and Los Angeles: University of California Press, 1991).

Piper, David, *The English Face* (Thames & Hudson, 1957).

Piper, David, *The Image of the Poet: British Poets and their Portraits* (Oxford: Clarendon Press, 1982).

Pliny, *Natural History*, trans. H. Rackham et al., 5 vols (Folio Society, 2012).

Pollard, Alfred William, *Titles and Colophons: Last Words on the History of the [Early] Title-Page with Notes on Some Colophons* (Nimmo, 1891; repr. Charleston, SC: Bibliobazaar, 2015).

Pollard, Alfred William, *Early Illustrated Books* (Kegan Paul, Trench, Trübner, 1893).

Pope, Alexander, *Poems*, ed. John Butt et al., 11 vols. in 12 (London: Methuen; New Haven: Yale University Press, 1939–69 ('Twickenham Pope').

Pope, Alexander, *The Correspondence*, ed. George Sherburn, 5 vols (Oxford: Clarendon Press, 1956).

Pope-Hennessy, John, *The Portrait in the Renaissance* (London: Phaidon Press; New York: Bollingen Foundation, 1966).

Praz, Mario, *Studies in Seventeenth-Century Imagery*, 2nd enlarged edn (Rome: Edizioni di Storia e Letteratura, 1964).

Praz, Mario, *The Flaming Heart* (New York: Doubleday, 1958).

Pugh, Syrithe, 'Ovidian Exile in the *Hesperides*: Herrick's Politics of Intertextuality', *Review of English Studies*, 57 (2006), 733–65.

Pugh, Syrithe, 'Supping with Ghosts: Imitation and Immortality in Herrick', in Ruth Connolly and Tom Cain (eds), *'Lords of Wine and Oile': Community and Conviviality in the Poetry of Robert Herrick* (Oxford: Oxford University Press, 2011), 220–49.

Puttenham, George, *The Art of English Poesy*, ed. Frank Whigham and Wayne A. Rebhorn (Ithaca, NY: Cornell University Press, 2007).

Ray, Gordon N., *The Illustrator and the Book in England from 1791 to 1914* (Oxford: Pierpont Morgan Library and Oxford University Press, 1976).

Riddell, James A., 'Ben Jonson's Folio of 1616', in Richard Harp and Stanley Stewart (eds), *The Cambridge Companion to Ben Jonson* (Cambridge: Cambridge University Press, 2000), 152–62.

Ripa, Cesare, *Iconologia* (Padua, 1611; facsimile edn, New York and London: Garland, 1976).

Rollin, Roger B., and Patrick, J. Max (eds), *'Trust to Good Verses': Herrick Tercentenary Essays* (Pittsburgh: University of Pittsburgh, 1978).

Rosenthal, Earl, *The Palace of Charles V in Granada* (Princeton: Princeton University Press, 1985).

Rosinus, Ioannes, *Antiquitatum romanorum corpus* [1583], ed. Thomas Dempster (1613).

Rosso Fiorentino, *Drawings, Prints, and Decorative Arts*, ed. Eugene A. Carroll (Washington: National Gallery of Art, 1987).

Russell, Daniel S., *The Emblem and Device in France* (Lexington, KY: French Forum, 1985).

Saenger, Michael, *The Commodification of Textual Engagements in the English Renaissance* (Aldershot and Burlington, VT: Ashgate, 2006).

Salter, Elizabeth, and Pearsall, Derek, 'Pictorial Illustration of Late Medieval Poetic Texts: The Role of the Frontispiece or Prefatory Picture', in Anderson et al. (eds), *Medieval Iconography and Narrative* (Odense: Odense University Press, 1980), 100–23.

Scher, Stephen K. (ed.), *The Currency of Fame: Portrait Medals of the Renaissance* (New York: Abrams and the Frick Collection, 1994).

Scott, William, *The Model of Poesy*, ed. Gavin Alexander (Cambridge: Cambridge University Press, 2013).

Sherman, William H., *John Dee: The Politics of Reading and Writing in the English Renaissance*, Massachusetts Studies in Early Medieval Culture (Amherst, MA: University of Massachusetts Press, 1995).

Sherman, William H., *Used Books: Marking Readers in Renaissance England* (Philadelphia, PA: University of Pennsylvania Press, 2008).

Shevlin, Eleanor F. '"To Reconcile Book and Title, and Make 'em Kin to One Another": The Evolution of the Title's Contractual Functions', *Book History*, 2 (1999), 42–77.

Sillars, Stuart, *The Illustrated Shakespeare 1709–1875* (Cambridge: Cambridge University Press, 2008).

Sisson, C. J., 'Grafton and the London Grey Friars', *Library*, 4th ser., 11 (1930), 121–49.

Smith, Helen, and Wilson, Louise (eds), *Renaissance Paratexts* (Cambridge: Cambridge University Press, 2011).

Smith, Margaret M., *The Title-Page: Its Early Development 1460–1510* (London: British Library; New Castle, DE: Oak Knoll Press, 2000).

Spence, Joseph, *Observations, Anecdotes and Characters of Books and Men*, ed. James M. Osborn, 2 vols (Oxford: Clarendon Press, 1966).

Spicer, Joaneath Ann, 'The Renaissance Elbow', in Jan Bremmer and Herman Roodenburg (eds), *A Cultural History of Gesture* (Cambridge: Polity; Ithaca, NY: Cornell University Press, 1992), 84–128.

Spielmann, M. H., *The Portraits of Geoffrey Chaucer*, Chaucer Soc., 2nd ser. no. 31 (Kegan Paul, Trench, Trübner for the Chaucer Society, 1900).

Spriggs, Gereth M., 'Unnoticed Bodleian Manuscripts, Illuminated by Herman Scheere and his School', *Bodleian Library Record*, 7 (1964), 193–203.

Stirling-Maxwell, Sir William, *Antwerp Delivered* […] *Illustrated with Facsimiles of Designs by Martin de Vos* […] (Edinburgh: David Douglas, 1878).

Stirling-Maxwell, Sir William, *The Chief Victories of* […] *Charles the Fifth, Designed by M. Heemskerck* (London and Edinburgh: privately printed for the editor, 1879).

Strutt, Joseph, *A Biographical Dictionary* […] *of* […] *Engravers*, 2 vols (1785–6).

Suarez, Michael F., SJ, and Woudhuysen, H. R., *The Oxford Companion to the Book*, 2 vols (Oxford: Oxford University Press, 2010).

Suckling, John, *Works*, ed. Thomas Clayton (Oxford: Clarendon Press, 1971).

Thomson, James, *The Complete Poetical Works*, ed. J. Logie Robertson (London: Oxford University Press, 1908).

Thurley, Simon, *The Building of England* (Collins, 2013).

Thynne, Francis, *Animadversions uppon the Annotacions* […] *of Chaucers Workes* […] *Reprinted in* […] *1598*, EETS, OS 9, rev. edn (1875; Oxford: Oxford University Press, 1965).

Tilley, Morris Palmer, *A Dictionary of the Proverbs in England in the Sixteenth and Seventeenth Centuries* (Ann Arbor, MI: University of Michigan Press, 1950).

Tonning, Erik (ed.), *Sightings: Selected Literary Essays* (New York: Peter Lang, 2008).

Tribble, Evelyn B., *Margins and Marginality: The Printed Page in Early Modern England* (Charlottesville, VA, and London: University Press of Virginia, 1993).

Vinne, Theodore Low de, *A Treatise on Title-Pages with Numerous Illustrations in Facsimile and some Observations on the Early and Recent Printing of Books* (New York: Century Co., 1902).

Virgil (Publius Vergilius Maro), *Opera*, ed. Sebastian Brant (Strasburg: Grieninger, 1502).

Walther, Ingo F., and Wolf, Norbert, *Codices Illustres: The World's Most Famous Illuminated Manuscripts 400 to 1600* (Cologne: Taschen, 2001).

West, William N., *Theatres and Encyclopedias in Early Modern Europe*. Cambridge Studies in Renaissance Literature and Culture (Cambridge: Cambridge University Press, 2003).

Whitney, Geoffrey, *A Choice of Emblems* (Leiden: Plantin, 1586; facsimile edn, ed. Henry Green, London: Lowell Green, 1866; repr. Hildesheim: Olms, 1971).

Wilson, F. P. (ed.), *Oxford Dictionary of English Proverbs*, 3rd edn (Oxford: Oxford University Press, 1970).

Wind, Edgar, *Pagan Mysteries in the Renaissance*, rev. edn (Faber, 1967).

Winternitz, Emanuel, *Musical Instruments and their Symbolism in Western Art* (Faber, 1967).

Wither, George, *A Collection of Emblems* (Robert Allot, 1635; facsimile edn, ed. John Horden, Menston: Scolar, 1968).

Wright, David H., *The Roman Vergil and the Origins of Medieval Book Design* (British Library, 2001).

Yates, Frances A., *The Art of Memory* (Routledge & Kegan Paul, 1966).

Yates, Frances A., *Theatre of the World* (Routledge & Kegan Paul, 1969).

Yates, Frances A., *Astraea: The Imperial Theme in the Sixteenth Century* (Routledge & Kegan Paul, 1975).

Young, Alan R., *Tudor and Jacobean Tournaments* (George Philip, 1987).

PICTURE CREDITS

INDEX

Figures are indicated by an italic *f* following the page number

Printed and bound by CPI Group (UK) Ltd, Croydon, CR0 4YY